THE SELECTION OF COLLEGE AND UNIVERSITY PRESIDENTS

By   Joseph F. Kauffman

ASSOCIATION OF AMERICAN COLLEGES
WASHINGTON, D.C.

1974

378.11
K162s

TABLE OF CONTENTS

Foreword 1
Introduction 3
Higher Education in the 1970's 7
The Governing Board 9
The Nature of the College and University Presidency Today 11
Characteristics of Present College and University Presidents 15
When a New President is to be Appointed 19
Organizing the Search Process 23
The Search Committee 27
The Search Process 33
    Qualifications and Criteria 35
    Obtaining Nominations and Candidates 39
        Affirmative Action 40
    Expanding the Search for Candidates 41
    Screening and Assessing Candidates 43
        Initial Screening 43
        References 44
        Interviews 44
Making the Final Decision 47
    Personal Inquiries of Associates 47
    Final Interviews 48
Making the Appointment 51
    Subjects to Cover 52
        Contract 52
        President's House 53
        President's Spouse 54
    Relationships with Board 56
    Criteria for Evaluation 57
    Career Development Concerns of Presidents 60
Presenting the New President 63
Epilogue 65
Notes 67
Bibliography 69
Appendix 71

Foreword

It is a truism that a great college or university is almost always the long shadow of a great leader—its president. Ironically, however, the process which is generally followed in recruiting and selecting the college president, as described in several recent "exposés," is itself often so haphazard as to be ludicrous.

This handbook has been prepared for the Association of American Colleges by Dr. Joseph F. Kauffman, Professor of Educational Administration, University of Wisconsin, Madison, with a grant from the Ford Foundation. Dr. Kauffman's approach to presidential selection is based on two principal assumptions. First, higher education has never before had so great a need for presidential leadership of the highest quality, a requirement that is likely to grow no less in the years immediately ahead. Second, improvement in the process of selection *can* contribute to the quality and effectiveness of that leadership.

Dr. Kauffman, himself a former college president, has witnessed the selection process in operation from both inside and out. Latterly, having returned to his preoccupations as scholar and teacher, he has subjected the process to a much needed critical evaluation. With the oversight of a task force composed of college and university presidents, he has produced a *vademecum* which should prove very useful to trustee and selection committees as well as to those prospective presidents who can find comfort and enlightenment from this glimpse behind the curtain of the selection process.

Frederic W. Ness, President
Association of American Colleges

© 1974, By
ASSOCIATION OF AMERICAN COLLEGES

All rights reserved, No part of this book may be reproduced in any form, by mimeograph or any other means, without permission in writing from the publishers.

L.C. Cat. Card No.: 74-18134

Introduction

This publication is written with an underlying premise: that the potential effectiveness of a college or university president is, at least in part, a function of the process by which he or she is selected. If that process involves the appropriate constituencies of the institution, clarifies goals, objectives and priorities, and enables the board to select a person it can support fully, then a foundation for success will have been established.

Effective educational leadership remains a crucial ingredient in the success of any higher education enterprise. Despite the pressing problems of finances and, in some cases, declining enrollments, our commitment to the fundamental value of learning must be constantly renewed. No one person or segment of an institution holds this trust exclusively. Yet it is the president who is expected to be the link among all of the parties involved. Governing boards, administrators, faculties, and students look to presidents not only to provide effective management but also to nourish the values for which institutions of higher learning stand.

Every year from two to three hundred colleges and universities face the necessity of choosing a new president. More and more that task has become complex, controversial, and difficult. Boards of trustees and regents often seek to learn from the experience of others and requests for specific guides are often sought. The role of the president is changing, and so is the role of governing boards, as constituent groups press for participation in the process of choosing a new leader.

Governing boards, administrators, faculties, and students look to presidents not only to provide effective management but also to nourish the values for which institutions of higher learning stand.

This publication is meant to be a guide for governing boards, search committees, and presidential aspirants. It describes the main ingredients in the process of selecting the chief executive of a college or university campus. It is meant to be instructive to all of the participants.

Obviously what follows in these pages should not be considered prescriptive for all. It is directed primarily to four-year colleges and universities, rather than two-year community colleges and junior colleges, although those institutions may find parts of it useful. It is meant for the selection of the chief executive officers of individual campuses, whether their title is president or chancellor. It is *not* meant for the selection of heads of state systems of higher education or heads of multi-campus systems, which may have quite different needs and objectives.

While the contents that follow are not prescriptive, they attempt to illuminate practices and principles that each institution will want to examine in creating its own presidential selection and appointment policies. They will have to be applied in ways appropriate to the individual differences among institutions.

Despite the concern of some observers with homogenization, American higher education still retains a remarkable diversity. There are some 2,900 colleges and universities throughout the United States. Excluding the two-year colleges, there are 543 public institutions and 1,284 private ones. They are large and small, public and private, urban and rural, independent and church-affiliated. With the possible exception of some colleges and universities controlled by religious orders, the material presented herein should be useful and generally applicable.

Following a brief comment on higher education in the 1970's, the topics covered include: The Governing Board, The Nature of the College Presidency Today, Characteristics of Present College and University Presidents, Organizing the Search Process, The Search Committee, Candidate Qualifications and Criteria, Obtaining Nominations and Candidates, Affirmative Action, Screening and Assessing Candidates, Making the Final Decision, The Appointment, Board-President Expectations and Relationships. Evaluation of Presidents and Career Development Concerns of Presidents are also treated.

Readers should note that the author's own references to the college or university president are expressed in terms that indicate such an office could be held by either a woman or a man. Because most of the writing about the college presidency assumes a male candidate or male incumbent, many of the quotations cited use the male pronoun. Such quotations may appear offensive to some readers but the language of the original source has not been altered.

Finally, I wish to make it clear that what follows represents the views of the author and is not an official statement of policy by the Association of American Colleges. The advice and counsel of the AAC Task Force on Presidential Selection and Career Development has been invaluable. Appreciation is expressed to the members of the Task Force: John W. Chandler, President, Williams College; Edward D. Eddy, Jr., President, Chatham College; Warren B. Knox (Chairman), Vice President for Public Affairs, Reed College; James M. Mitchell, Member of Board of Directors and Past Chairman, Association of Governing Boards of Universities and Colleges; Barbara Newell, President, Wellesley College; Edgar F. Shannon, President, University of Virginia; and Marvin Wachman, President, Temple University. The generosity of the Ford Foundation in making this publication possible is gratefully acknowledged.

I am also appreciative of the wisdom and support received from the AAC staff, including President Frederic W. Ness, Elden Smith and John Gillis, and the editorial assistance of Marti Patchell. Of course, final responsibility for the contents must be borne solely by the author. Like other former college presidents, he knows that all credit is to be widely shared but the responsibility is his alone.

Joseph F. Kauffman

Madison, Wisconsin
August, 1974

Higher Education in the 1970's

Institutions of higher education function in a social context which requires understanding as we define institutional objectives and select our leaders. While there is ample opportunity to challenge the trends of the times or to move counter to the conventional wisdom, it is necessary to take into account where higher education has been and where it may be going.

After a period of unprecedented growth and optimism, our colleges and universities have entered a period of stabilization and, for some, retrenchment. Some institutions face enormous financial difficulties, and reductions in faculty and staff are not uncommon. Public attitudes toward higher education are changing and government reassesses the level of its support along with other pressing social priorities. New demands and expectations for economy, sound management and accountability equal or exceed earlier pressures for a socially relevant curriculum, student participation and new program development.

In the thrust for more effective management, new conflicts occur. Programs must be reviewed, priorities set, and effectiveness evaluated. New techniques of management are becoming crucial, yet they need to be recognized as means, not ends. Both the public and the academy are still having difficulty in agreeing upon the essential purposes of higher education.

Higher education has accepted many functions now crucial to American society. Because access to higher education is seen as vital to social and economic opportunity, it has become an expectation. Who shall pay for it and who benefits from it remain areas of public debate. Yet it seems clear that college attendance will continue to be the main path for upward mobility. The nature of aid to students and institutions will continue to be debated.

Both the public and the academy are still having difficulty in agreeing upon the essential purposes of higher education.

Private colleges and universities will be challenged, as never before, to develop distinctive purposes and programs to attract students and financial support. Without such uniqueness, ability to compete with the low-tuition institutions of the public sector is limited.

Public institutions, and their forms of governance, are becoming increasingly responsive to public authority. In some ways, public colleges and universities are being regarded as state agencies and the advent of academic collective bargaining may accelerate this trend. The allocation of public resources for public higher education has become an integral part of the political process. In such a setting, effective political leadership becomes a crucial qualification for those who would head public institutions.

The college president should provide the knowledge and leadership to guide the institution in its responses to the challenges and opportunities it faces.

There is considerable writing available on the problems facing higher education, most notably the voluminous published reports of the Carnegie Commission on Higher Education. Each institution must take this backdrop into account as it goes about setting its own plans and objectives for the remainder of the decade. Each college and university will have to make difficult choices and decisions in the years ahead. Governing boards and those responsible for goal-setting and policy decisions require an awareness of the total fabric of higher education.

The college president should provide the knowledge and leadership to guide the institution in its responses to the challenges and opportunities it faces.

The Governing Board

Effective governance of a college or university requires a sound relationship between governing board and president. To find, and retain, a president with the qualities necessary to lead their institution, is one of the most important responsibilities of trusteeship.

In the sections that follow frequent reference will be made to boards of trustees, regents or governing boards. Whatever its title, the governing board of a college or university normally serves as the repository of final institutional authority.

> **Effective governance of a college or university requires a sound relationship between governing board and president. To find, and retain, a president with the qualities necessary to lead their institution, is one of the most important responsibilities of trusteeship.**

Contrary to practices in many other countries, American colleges and universities are governed by boards of lay citizens in which legal authority and liability are lodged. Space does not permit portraying the history of governing boards, although an understanding of that history is valuable for board members and presidents. Since education is a responsibility of the states rather than the federal government, they are empowered to grant charters for the establishment of colleges and universities. A private institution, seeking such a charter, must have a corporate identity which centers in a board. Similarly, a public institution, whether created constitutionally or statutorily, requires a body of citizens to implement its purposes and protect the public trust.

During the two decades following World War II, governing boards delegated considerable authority to presidents and faculties. Systems of academic self-governance were developed, implementing a concept which came to be known as "shared authority." This concept was enunciated nationally in the 1966 *Statement on Government of Colleges and Universities,* jointly formulated by the American Association of University Professors, the American Council on Education and the Association of Governing Boards of Universities and Colleges. This statement speaks of the "inescapable interdependence among governing board, administration, faculty, students and others."[1]

Governing board members are aware that their roles are often ambiguous. Ideally, they should concern themselves with matters of policy and avoid getting into administrative details. However, the line separating the two is frequently blurred. They are expected to react to recommendations brought before them rather than to initiate recommendations. Some argue that they ought to deal only with financial and budgetary matters rather than academic questions. Yet we have learned that financial policy has significant impact on academic policy questions. Further, educational policy may be a crucial determinant in attracting or discouraging student enrollment. Such matters cannot be divorced from an institution's fiscal policies.

There has been a great change in the mood and concerns of board members in recent years and moves to strengthen the role of governing boards can be seen. Student disruption, obstruction and violence resulted in public cries of "Who's in charge?" Parents, legislators, alumni and donors called for the assertion of the legal authority held by governing boards. The severe financial problems now being experienced call for skillful management of resources and greater accountability. Governing boards are ultimately held accountable, despite their unpaid status. Thus, in more and more institutions, governing boards have moved from *pro forma* approval of the president's recommendations to a full involvement in the issues confronting their campuses. Board members, too, have relationships with constituencies both on and off campus.

With these changes, and other concerns on the horizon, governing boards have taken on enormous burdens. Their concept of the presidency, and of the president's relationship to the board and its members, becomes a crucial ingredient when leadership succession must be faced by an institution.

Governing boards are no longer fully dependent on the president for information and awareness of educational matters confronting our colleges and universities. They subscribe to *The Chronicle of Higher Education*, *Change* magazine, and *AGB Reports*. They read Carnegie Commission publications, and they attend conferences sponsored by the Association of Governing Boards of Universities and Colleges, an increasingly important association of over 610 member governing boards, with some 13,000 trustees or regents, on 960 campuses in the United States.

With these changes, and other concerns on the horizon, governing boards have taken on enormous burdens. Their concept of the presidency, and of the president's relationship to the board and its members, becomes a crucial ingredient when leadership succession must be faced by an institution.

The Nature of the College and University Presidency Today

A separate publication would be required to deal adequately with the changing nature of the presidency of an American college or university. To discuss the selection of a president, and the process of selection, however, requires some portrayal of the changing conceptions of the office.

Many published memoirs illustrate a wide variety of presidential roles over various periods of history. There are many different views on the nature of the office of president. In some ways portrayals of the presidency even a quarter-century ago seem oddly quaint to those who know its reality today.

In the foreword to a recent study of the college presidency sponsored by the Carnegie Commission on Higher Education, Clark Kerr states, "In the view of this study, one of the major characteristics of the presidency of an American college or university is ambiguity. One of the greatest of the ambiguities relates to what the president is supposed to be: a sound manager with a balanced budget, a successful 'colonial' administrator who can keep the 'natives' quiet, a moral leader attacking evil, or any one of a number of other things."[2]

There are many ascriptions and characterizations of college presidents. Although these have changed over the years, aspects of the old blend with the contemporary. Thorstein Veblen's phrase, "captains of erudition," sounds strangely dated today, but one can find in the literature an ample supply of cryptic, descriptive phrases such as "fund-raiser," "mediator," "persuader," "innovator," and the like.

Some of the more recent conceptions of the presidency are cited below to illustrate the differences in expectations regarding the role.

> *Those who enjoy it are not very successful, and those who are successful are not very happy. The explanation is hidden somewhere in the philosophy of power. Those who enjoy exercising power shouldn't have it, and those who should exercise it are not likely to enjoy it. One thing is clear: colleges must have presidents and it makes a great difference who they are. (Harold W. Stoke)*[3]

> *The campus leader today is a mediator, a negotiator, and a man who jockeys between power blocs, trying to carve out viable futures for his institution. Unlike the autocratic president who ruled with an iron hand, the contemporary academic president finds that he must play the political role by pulling together coalitions to fight for desired changes. The academic monarch of yesteryear has almost vanished and in his place has come not the academic 'bureaucrat,' as many suggest, but the academic 'statesman.' (J. Victor Baldridge)*[4]

> *The world may collapse tomorrow; it may not. The University may survive another ten years; it may not. The differences are important, and the problems are serious. But the outcomes do not much depend on the college president. He is human. His capabilities are limited, and his responsibility is limited by his capabilities. We believe there are modest gains to be made by making some changes in the perception of his role. We believe presidents can be more effective and relaxed. We do not believe in magic. (Michael D. Cohen and James G. March)*[5]
>
> *The major discovery that emerged from the explorations of the last five days is that significant innovation cannot take place within the University without the active support and leadership of the president. There is no substitute for presidential leadership, and a president who merely presides over his institution will find himself presiding over an anachronism—and sooner or later a dissolving one. Most presidents have more opportunities than they make use of to influence their institutions. . . . In the increasing difficulties in which universities find themselves today, the role, or rather the many roles of the president are ever more critical.*
>
> *Because of the multiplicity of these roles, one is tempted to highlight the traditional brokerage function of the president, or his role as protector of the institution against press attacks and legislative budget cuts. It is true that the faculty is more anxious to see the president bring home the bacon, than to see him calling on them in their offices. But if the central weakness of the university today is its loss of a firm sense of institutional purpose then the central role of the president must be to articulate that purpose. He must do so in ways that will marshal the most resolute elements in all his constituencies, and raise a standard to which the brave and honest can repair. (Workshop on "Presidential Leadership and University Change")*[6]

Whatever one's conception of the contemporary college and university president, it appears that there are changing roles, functions and expectations. In public institutions governing boards can no longer act solely as advocates of their institutions. They must also represent the public and receive and act on petitions, complaints and demands for responsiveness. Faculty, staff, and students are less and less willing to have the president speak for them and insist upon direct access to boards and political leaders who can effect change. The advent of collective bargaining adds a new dimension to the picture, which further confounds the traditional role of the president as spokesman for the campus. Competing and conflicting interests, and demands for public accountability, lead to a more political style of management.

Cohen and March, in their book on the presidency, report on the descriptive images of the presidency which they developed from a series of role-similarity judgments made by the 42 presidents in their sample. In personal interviews, held in the spring of 1970, the presidents were asked to rate seven occupational roles in terms of their similarity to the role of a college or university president. The other occupations were: mayor, business

---

Increasingly, the job of the president is seen as requiring both political leadership and the skills of the executive.

---

executive, bookkeeper, foreman, military commander, clergyman, and labor-management mediator. The analysis of responses showed that college and university presidents saw the role of "mayor" as most similar, with "business executive" a close second.[7]

Increasingly, the job of the president is seen as requiring both political leadership and the skills of the executive.

Characteristics of Present College and University Presidents

A number of studies have examined pre-presidential career patterns, factors of age and academic background, and length of tenure in office. Several of these (Bolman, Cohen and March, Ferrari, Hodgkinson, Kerr, Selden) are listed in the bibliography of this publication. In their study, Cohen and March synthesize much of the earlier work and add some unique contributions of their own. Their chapter on Presidential Tenure is a major contribution.

Cohen and March estimate the average age of presidents now in the office to be about 53.

The average age of those entering a college presidency seems to have varied only slightly over the past several decades. In 1964, Bolman reported an average beginning age to be 46 years. Ferrari, surveying presidents selected in 1967-68, found the average age to be 45.6 years.

Typically, presidents begin their academic careers as college teachers. They later become department chairpersons, moving from that responsibility to deanships or similar administrative posts on the way to becoming presidents. Although some persons do move directly from a faculty position to a presidency, particularly in smaller colleges, the vast majority of newly appointed presidents have had substantial previous administrative experience. In most cases, this administrative experience was at an institution other than the one at which the office of president is attained.*

The length of a president's term of office, or the tenure expectancy of presidents, is a subject of much speculation. During the years of student disruption, and the advent of new community colleges, the media highlighted the many vacancies in terms of "presidencies going begging."

Presently there seems to be an expectation that presidents will stay in office fewer years than heretofore. Although presidents serve "at the pleasure of the board," and may be terminated accordingly, some institutions are adopting limited terms of office usually with a possibility of reappointment. Five to ten years now seems to be the normal expectation for presidential tenure. In personal interviews conducted in 1970 in their study of the presidency, Cohen and March found that presidents themselves felt their tenure should be seven to ten years (unless they had already exceeded that figure). This was reinforced by the responses of the people around presidents

---

*The author's examination of the positions of newly-appointed presidents over a 12-month period in 1973-74 reveals that 75% were from administrative positions *outside* the institution at which the presidency was attained.

(trustees, faculty, subordinates and students) who also saw a norm of seven to ten-year terms for presidents.*

Clark Kerr provides some interesting data concerning the presidents of the most prestigious doctoral-granting universities in our country, the 48 members of the Association of American Universities. In 1899, the average years in office of this group of presidents was 10.9 years. By 1969 this had dropped to 5.9. Because averages can be misleading, owing to a small number of long-service individuals, Kerr also computed "median years of experience" and found that the median had dropped from 7 years in 1929 to 2 years in 1969.[8]

Cohen and March do not discover any evidence of major recent changes in the expected tenure of new presidents. They do find that there has been a significant long-term decline in the tenure of presidents of large universities. They also believe that rapid growth of an institution tends to reduce presidential tenure while relative stability in size tends to increase tenure. Most of all, they feel there has been an underestimation of the importance of age and tenure norms.

> *Presidents are much more likely to leave at about age 50 than they are at ages 43 or 57. Presidential departures are also keyed to length of service in a way that suggests an implicit term of office that is five years long (with decreasing prospects of renewal). Here as elsewhere in our investigation of the presidential role, we observe the apparent impact of social expectations in the regulation of life.*

* * *

> *Part of the reason that presidents leave the presidency at a relatively rapid rate around age 50 is that they reach the age of last opportunity, after which the quality of jobs for which they qualify starts to deteriorate rapidly.*[9]

Presidential departure highlights an interesting problem to which we shall return in discussing the nature of the appointment and the relationships between governing board and president. The fact is that presidents are assuming office earlier and must consider post-presidential careers while undergoing

---

*One informal measure of presidential tenure in office was conducted by the author when he received a copy of the Cohen and March book on the presidency, *Leadership and Ambiguity: The American College President*. As one of the 42 college and university presidents in the national sample surveyed under the auspices of the Carnegie Commission on Higher Education, I eagerly read the results. I also looked at the names of the other 41 presidents who had been visited and interviewed in the Spring of 1970 when the study was begun. A quick check of the 42 names, based entirely on my personal knowledge of job changes, retirements or resignations revealed that 45% of those in the sample were no longer in their presidencies by the time the book was published in December, 1973.

the rigors of the presidency. Governing boards must take such facts into account in appointing and nurturing the leaders they select to guide and guard their institutions.

The fact is that presidents are assuming office earlier and must consider post-presidential careers while undergoing the rigors of the presidency. Governing boards must take such facts into account in appointing and nurturing the leaders they select to guide and guard their institutions.

The post-presidential career concerns of presidents will be discussed in the section on "Making The Appointment."

When a New President is to be Appointed

Although some colleges and universities have formal policy statements, or by-laws, covering the steps to be taken when a presidential vacancy occurs, for many others the event results in a period of crisis. The process of leadership succession in higher education seems less well-developed than in other organizations and is often a source of considerable conflict.

In a recent study of presidential succession, John Steiner suggests that "the formal and informal procedures of presidential selection in colleges and universities have much in common with procedures of leadership selection used by other complex, pluralistic organizations such as nations, legislatures, corporations, peak associations, and international organizations." To be effective Steiner believes the selection process must "gain the consensus of groups which might veto the leader."[10]

Robert Birnbaum, recently appointed chancellor of the Oshkosh campus in the University of Wisconsin System, contrasts the leadership succession process in business with that of higher education. He believes that "while business firms utilize anticipatory recruitment, in-service socialization, and internal promotions within a bureaucratic framework, colleges and universities generally select presidents from other academic institutions using informal and *ad hoc* processes."[11]

Governing boards which do not now have provisions in their code or by-laws covering the procedures to be followed in the event of a presidential vacancy should develop such policies. It is important for the board to indicate clearly its authority to make the appointment, and of equal importance perhaps, to indicate that it will determine the process by which constituent groups will be invited to participate in the search for a new president.

The *ad hoc* nature of the presidential selection process in higher education and the fact that the appointing authority, the governing board, must attempt to gain a consensus of the various constituent groups, may generate unforeseen conflict.

Governing boards which do not now have provisions in their code or by-laws covering the procedures to be followed in the event of a presidential vacancy should develop such policies. It is important for the board to indicate clearly its authority to make the appointment, and of equal importance perhaps, to indicate that it will determine the *process* by which constituent groups will be invited to participate in the search for a new president.

> **Whenever possible, a governing board should announce the search and selection procedures which will be followed at the same meeting that it formally acts upon a presidential resignation or retirement.**

If an unexpected vacancy occurs, without such policies having been set, there may be considerable conflict over what procedures ought to be followed. A vacuum can be created in which challenges to the legitimacy of the interim arrangements, and the selection process itself, may engender considerable ill-will and dysfunctional pressures. Whenever possible, a governing board should announce the search and selection procedures which will be followed *at the same meeting* that it formally acts upon a presidential resignation or retirement. Obviously this will be difficult if a president's departure is unplanned or a surprise to the board itself. Unless there are ill-feelings with its president, a board should have as much as a year's notice of plans to resign or retire. In such cases the board may delay public notice of the president's planned departure until it is ready to announce the plans it has formulated for selecting a successor.

In many cases, a governing board will also have to make interim arrangements for the administration of the institution, designating someone as an interim or acting president. It will also have to decide what role, if any, to give the outgoing president, in the process of searching for a successor.

Some institutions may need to take a long, penetrating look at themselves before deciding what kind of new leadership they require. Frederic W. Ness has suggested that an *ad hoc* or interim president, preferably from outside, be engaged for a limited period in such cases. Such a person would have no expectation or aspiration for a permanent appointment. He or she would provide for the continuing management of the institution. More importantly, such a person would help the board and the college community chart their future course so that they could then search for a new president to lead them in their desired direction.[12]

Sometimes circumstances will require the designation of an acting president for a brief period. Normally, the chief academic officer will be so designated if a temporary leader is required. However, the person designated acting president should not be one who is an active candidate for the presidency, especially if the college or university wishes to attract other outside candidates for the position. The acting president will be a major source of information about the institution for candidates who are to be interviewed on campus. It is a serious omission not to have the acting president participate in these interviews. Yet, if this person is also an active candidate for the position an awkward situation results.

Obviously, a governing board will want to enable persons from inside the institution to become candidates for the presidency if they choose to do so. Yet, in some circumstances, inside candidates have some liabilities, including the fact that their weaknesses, unlike outside candidates, are known. They may also be identified with one or more of the factions inside the institution vying for influence in the final decision. This can become a source of conflict among the groups participating in the search.

It is also recommended that the outgoing president be completely detached from the selection process. Although he or she may be helpful to the governing board in the development of search and screening procedures, the outgoing president should not be in a position of selecting a successor.

In considering the question of an inside or outside candidate, the governing board will have to decide the current and future needs of the institution. The ultimate choice should depend on who best meets those needs.

It is also recommended that the outgoing president be completely detached from the selection process. Although he or she may be helpful to the governing board in the development of search and screening procedures, the outgoing president should not be in a position of selecting a successor.

The period immediately following the resignation of a president is a difficult one. Joseph M. Ray, a former university president, described it well when he said, "It is a period when temporary consternation and concern, and delight as well on the part of some, give way to an ever-deepening sense of marking time until the new president is selected and arrives on the scene."[13]

Organizing the Search Process

"Today's presidential search is an Easter egg hunt: many people want to participate, and thousands want to watch."[14]

The search process associated with selecting presidents at most colleges and universities is, at best, a compromise. Although authority to make the final choice and the appointment is clearly in the hands of the governing board, in most cases the faculty, students, alumni and others will expect to be consulted.

The concept of "shared authority" presumes consultation with the faculty. The previously mentioned *Statement on Government of Colleges and Universities* contains the following statement concerning the search:

> Joint efforts of a most critical kind must be taken when an institution chooses a new president. The selection of a chief administrative officer should follow upon cooperative search by the governing board and the faculty, taking into consideration the opinion of others who are appropriately interested. The president should be equally qualified to serve both as the executive officer of the governing board and as the chief academic officer of the institution and the faculty. His dual role requires that he be able to interpret to board and faculty the educational views and concepts of institutional government of the other. He should have the confidence of the board and the faculty.[15]

Many observers have commented on the search process. Some view the search process as a mess while others see it as a unique opportunity. Frederic W. Ness describes the process in the following manner: "Of all the capricious, disorganized, unprofessional operations in human society, this one would certainly appear to qualify for some kind of negative award."[16]

Robert M. Hyde sees the search process as an opportunity ". . . for those boards who are willing at the outset to plan and organize it well and pursue it with diligence, it can be an exceptional opportunity to strengthen the institution in several important ways. It can be the vehicle for providing new insights and understanding of the institution, improving relations with faculty and staff, and promoting increased support from outside sources. And the search that generates these important by-products has the best possible chance of launching a successful and productive presidency!"[17]

Father Paul Reinert, former president and now chancellor of St. Louis University, bemoans the new emphasis on widespread participation in the search process. He observes that ". . . while the powers, prerogatives and, to some extent, prestige of the college president have steadily eroded, the process by which new presidents are chosen has never been more complex and meticulous." Father Reinert states that ". . . once you try to involve a lot of people in the search process, there is no end to it. Either you wind up with one huge committee or an impossible collection of small committees—and either way the result is a managerial headache of major proportions."[18]

John Steiner believes that the selection process, although criticized as *ad hoc*, slow, cumbersome, inefficient, and undemocratic, is a functional and pragmatic institutional response because it focuses attention on the role of the university and reconciles competing elements both inside and outside the campus political community.

Steiner summarizes his thesis this way:

> *In selecting a man, the committee must first ascertain what role the man will have to play before the members can ascertain what talents and qualifications to look for in a nominee. And before settling on the one man who will be the future president, the committee must determine that the new president and what he stands for will be acceptable to important constituent and audience groups in the university milieu. In this way, the mechanism for the selection of leadership is related to the specific leadership role.*[19]

It becomes evident that each institution will have to create the search process which best meets its own needs. A small institution may use a very simple process. One such college, known to the author, had a disastrous experience with an outside appointee. When that person stepped down, under pressure from the faculty and the board, there was a clear consensus for the appointment of a highly respected insider who had been academic dean and vice-president for a number of years. The process was abbreviated and the appointment promptly made to the pleasure of all the concerned constituencies. This is, of course, a rare occurrence.

Public institutions have many requirements and obligations which often dictate an extensive, open process in both the search and selection.

Whatever process is used to search for the new president, it should clearly be under the control of the governing board. Further, it should be related to the institution's own, often unique, circumstances, problems and opportunities.

A variety of procedures and techniques employed in both public and private institutions will be described in the following pages. Whatever process is used to search for the new president, it should clearly be under the control of the governing board. Further, it should be related to the institution's own, often unique, circumstances, problems and opportunities. The qualifications sought in a president should relate to the specific needs of the institution as determined by the board, in consultation with the faculty and other constituencies of the college or university.

Some institutions may benefit from the use of an outside consultant to guide them in the search process. Outside consultants cannot, of course, do the work of the governing board or replace the participation of the key constituencies of the institution. A danger, also, is that some within the institution will resent the obvious influence of "outsiders." Nevertheless, professional counsel may be helpful in those cases where the lack of experience and confidence warrant such assistance.

There are some private consulting firms which provide services in connection with the search for college presidents. On a fixed fee basis these consultants aid governing boards and search committees in defining the institution's needs, outlining the characteristics of the kind of person the institution should be seeking, provide a staff person for the committee, suggest techniques for obtaining desirable nominations, suggest names of possible candidates, conduct background investigations on selected candidates and aid in the public relations of the actual appointment. Assistance in any or all of these matters may be necessary or helpful for some colleges or universities.

There is a difference between asking for advice and turning over the whole job to a management consulting firm or agency. Each governing board seeking assistance has to assess its own unique needs so that it will not purchase more than is required. Professional counsel may be useful in speeding up the search process, in identifying and obtaining information on candidates, or in selling a desirable candidate on the possibilities of an institution. A board which recognizes a need for guidance in an administrative reorganization may wish to combine such a task with plans for a presidential search.

There are also disadvantages in using outside counsel. They may not really understand the ambience or needs of the institution and thus offend important elements among the constituencies. Also they can be expensive, in comparison with the "free" services which most board and faculty committees provide. Further, they may not fully appreciate the value of participation by the various constituencies of an institution in the selection process.

If a board employs a consulting agency, it should make clear what limits have been set on the consultant's task. The board must retain its full authority to make the actual selection and appointment of the president.

The Search Committee

There is no more important responsibility for a governing board than the selection and appointment of a new president. No matter what arrangements have been created to involve others, the election of the president should be accomplished by action of the full membership of the governing board.

Before describing several different presidential selection models that have been used recently in public and private institutions, it is necessary to clarify the different words that are used to describe committee functions. These functions include the *search* for candidates, the *screening* of candidates, the *selection* of a short list of recommended finalists or a single, best qualified candidate and, finally *appointing* the new president.

There is no more important responsibility for a governing board than the selection and appointment of a new president. No matter what arrangements have been created to involve others, the election of the president should be accomplished by action of the full membership of the governing board.

The *selection* of presidents is normally in the hands of the governing board or a committee of the governing board specifically empowered to present their choice. On some campuses, mainly private institutions, the governing board may appoint trustees, representatives of the faculty, students and alumni on a single selection committee empowered to search, screen and select the president. The board would appoint the person selected. Warren Bennis, whose writing on this subject has been lively and provocative, has recommended that the search and selection authority be in the hands of one representative committee. However, this is not the typical practice.[20]

The more typical pattern is for the governing board, or the board's own selection committee, to establish a sub-committee or advisory committee, comprised of representatives of the faculty, students and other constituencies. Such a sub-committee may carry the designation *search committee, search and screen committee* or *advisory committee*. Its functions may include conducting the actual searching for and screening of candidates, recommending a short list of approved candidates to the selection committee of the board, or offering observations on the qualified candidates the board has identified and participating in their interviews.

The governing board must decide on the procedures it wishes to follow and must be in charge of the process. If stated procedures do not exist they ought to be created and set forth in writing at the outset to avoid the conflict and tensions that can arise as the process unfolds.*

> **A rationale for representation and for the limits of participation ought to be developed if one does not exist.**

The governing board must also decide which constituent groups will be asked to participate in a consultative or advisory role in the various stages of the search. A rationale for representation and for the limits of participation ought to be developed if one does not exist. The question of representation for various pressure and interest groups can become a divisive force, diverting the board from the main objective—selecting the most competent person it can find to lead their institution.

It is recommended that the search and screening committee, whatever its designated name, be broadly representative of all the major constituencies with which a new president will have to function. Obviously, this means that the faculty will have significant representation. Plans should also be made for student and alumni participation. Some institutions, because of their nature, will want to include representatives of the community. The board should designate the chairperson of the committee.

> **It is recommended that the search and screening committee, whatever its designated name, be broadly representative of all the major constituencies with which a new president will have to function.**

One recently appointed president of a private institution noted that he was selected solely by a board committee. In retrospect he observed, "I believe it would have been well had there been student and faculty members on the committee. I am not at all sure that the outcome would have been different. However, it might have been helpful in smoothing the sailing within the institution."

---

*A recent publication by the American Council on Education, *Selecting Academic Administrators: The Search Committee*, by Richard A. Kaplowitz, is a brief but adequate review of desirable procedures and practices. Although it is meant primarily for selecting chairpersons, directors of programs, deans and vice-presidents, its contents will be especially useful in showing all of the major steps in the search process.

Deciding who will represent the various constituent groups on the search or selection committee should be a part of the formal procedure. If the appropriate bodies exist, such as Faculty Senates, Student Councils and Alumni Association Boards, they can be asked to select representatives. If not, other arrangements can be made for the formal election or appointment of representatives. Some boards insist on receiving names of nominees, from faculty, student and alumni groups, reserving to the board itself the actual appointment of the committee members. Whatever the method used, it should result in an adequately representative advisory committee. If not, the governing board should supplement the committee's membership on its own authority. The committee should, as appropriate, include women and minority representation.*

Five different approaches to the search process are described here to illustrate the similar ingredients in the process as well as differences among various types of institutions. In the Appendix will be found more complete descriptions of the search and selection process for new presidents, utilized recently, at these five colleges and universities: (1) Culver-Stockton College (Missouri); (2) Mankato State College (Minnesota); (3) California State University and Colleges; (4) University of Wisconsin; and (5) Knox College (Illinois).

(1) Culver-Stockton College is a private institution in Canton, Missouri, affiliated with the Christian Church (Disciples of Christ). The governing board appointed a search committee of six of its members, designating one member as Chairman. That search committee established its own procedures, including the creation of a sub-committee of faculty and student representatives. That sub-committee participated with the search committee in formulating a description of the position, the screening of the credentials of candidates, and developing a short list of semi-finalist candidates.

The search committee, itself, interviewed the choices from the short list and decided on a preferred candidate which it presented to the full board for election to the presidency. Every effort was made to avoid any division between board, faculty and students throughout the process.

(2) Mankato State College, Minnesota, used the formal procedures of The Minnesota State College Board in the search for and selection of its new president. The Board, responsible for seven state colleges, has its own executive officer for the system—a Chancellor.

---

*The author recalls the problems of the board of regents in creating a campus advisory committee to participate in the search for his successor. At one board meeting, two months following his resignation, more than two hours were spent by the board considering who would represent the faculty—the faculty council's designees or those of the AFT, which had just won a collective bargaining election. Further it received and debated the petition of black faculty and staff which sought a separate representative on the committee.

A Presidential Search Committee, made up of campus representatives served in an advisory capacity to the Chancellor and the State College Board. Although the written administrative procedure calls for this committee to be comprised of no more than thirteen persons, representing faculty, students, staff and alumni, in actuality the Mankato State College search committee ended up with thirty-one members. The Committee was chaired by the Vice-Chancellor for Academic Affairs, an officer of the central administration, as differentiated from the campus administration. Leadership for reducing the pool of applicants to a manageable number of the most highly qualified was clearly in the hands of the chairperson. Nevertheless, the Committee could also introduce names to the list.

From the short list of semi-finalist candidates, the Chancellor invited three persons for interviews. These on-campus interviews made the candidates available to the representatives of various campus groups. An advisory group of community representatives also interviewed the candidates.

Finally, each candidate was interviewed, publicly, by members of the State College Board and Chancellor, with news media present. The Chairman of the Committee forwarded all comments to the Chancellor who recommended a nominee to the Board for appointment to the Presidency of Mankato State College.

Note that in this public institution a large, diverse campus committee, plus a community advisory committee were included in the process. Interviews with the governing board were held in public, in accordance with a new state law. The successful candidate in the search was asked by the author how he felt about the public aspects of the process. He replied, "Mature people in or seeking public positions should be able both to participate in and tolerate public deliberations. The Board members were respectful and compassionate and yet asked direct and appropriate questions. It may have been tougher on them than on me," he added. In summary, he noted "the Board interview was a picnic compared to the marathon on-campus interviews."

Obviously some outstanding persons will not choose to become candidates in such an open, competitive process. Yet in some institutions, and state systems, the political and legal requirements are such that a process of this type is necessary if the new president is to be granted the legitimacy needed to be an effective leader.

(3) The California State University and Colleges System comprises nineteen campuses, each of which is headed by a President. The System is governed by a single Board of Trustees. The chief executive officer of the System is a Chancellor.

Whenever a presidential vacancy occurs on a campus within the system, the Chancellor and the Chairman of the Board of Trustees establishes a Presidential Selection Advisory Committee. This Committee consists of three representatives of the campus, two trustees, one president from another campus in the system, one member of the Advisory Board of the campus, a staff person from the central administration and the Chancellor. This is sometimes referred to as a "rainbow committee."

All contacts with candidates, including background studies of finalists are handled by the Vice-Chancellor for Faculty and Staff Affairs, in the System's central administration. The Committee decides, on the basis of information provided, whom it wishes to interview. The process culminates with the Chancellor recommending a final candidate to the Board of Trustees.

The policy and procedures of the California State University and Colleges System have been under attack recently by the faculty and academic senates of the individual institutions within the System. The conflict became a matter of public record in the 1973 selection process of the President of California State University, San Francisco. Following leaks to the press concerning the names of the finalist candidates and other conflicts, the Chairman of the Board of Trustees dismissed the official presidential selection advisory committee. The Board appointed a new president some six weeks later and the Academic Senate of the San Francisco campus he was to head passed a resolution asking the new President to withdraw. He continues to serve.

One of the main objections of the Academic Senate was that all contact with the candidates and all background and reference checks were restricted to the Chancellor's staff. Campus faculty representatives were not permitted to investigate candidates on their own. At this writing, the Statewide Academic Senate is pressing for a revision in the procedures to provide a greater faculty role on each campus.

(4) Although the University of Wisconsin is a large and complex system comprising 27 campuses, with a single governing board (Board of Regents), search procedures are highly decentralized. A President heads this system, and Chancellors administer individual campuses.

Upon notice of a vacancy a Special Regent Committee, working with the System President produces a brief description of the position that is to become open. The System President then appoints a Search and Screen Committee comprised of a majority of faculty but including students and staff. The System President appoints the chairperson of the Committee.

Solicitation of nominations and applications, screening of credentials and interviews are all handled by the Search and Screen Committee which, subsequently, recommends a list of at least five individuals to the System President.

Recommended candidates are evaluated and interviewed by the System President in cooperation with the Special Regent Committee. From this process, a single candidate is recommended to the Board of Regents for appointment.

(5) Knox College, Galesburg, Illinois, is a small, private college which was led for 24 years by Dr. Sharvy G. Umbeck who died in 1973. In searching for his successor, the trustees of Knox College created a Search Committee of fifteen members. The Committee included nine trustees, three faculty mem-

bers, two students and the Acting President of the College. Because the trustee members were from a wide geographical area, those persons from the campus area became a form of "sub-committee," performing a substantial part of the information-gathering and checking of references.

Some nine months were required to complete the search process at Knox College. More than 200 names were considered before the Committee decided on a short list of twelve candidates to interview. Three finalists came to the campus for one and one-half day periods each, meeting with faculty, staff and students. At the conclusion of these campus visits, a choice was made.

From the above illustrations, it is clear that a variety of procedures and practices exist for constituting search, screening and selection committees. Private institutions may have flexibility in resolving such matters, yet in almost all cases some participation or consultation is afforded faculty and student representatives.

The Search Process

Once the procedures have been settled, authority for conduct of the search clarified, and an appropriate committee or committees appointed, the process of finding suitable nominees or candidates commences. Clearly, the role of the chairperson of the governing board has been crucial up to this point and continues to be one of leadership, especially in single campus institutions. Even where a member of the governing board has been designated chairperson of a search committee, candidates will look to the head of the governing board for clarification of most issues. Continuing liaison activity will be required between the committees and the governing board, for it is the board which will make the ultimate appointment.

The objectives of the search process are to: (1) clarify the requirements of the institution regarding the nature of its presidential leadership; (2) develop a statement of qualifications and criteria for the position based upon these needs; (3) solicit nominations and candidates from a wide variety of sources; (4) develop an orderly and objective procedure for assessing the candidates; (5) screen the most qualified candidates; and (6) submit to those with the final selection authority a recommended list of outstanding candidates acceptable to the various constituencies represented on the search committee. From this point on, the governing board, or its selection committee, conducts final background investigations, reference checks, sometimes on-site visits and personal interviews in reaching its decision on one candidate.

A minimum of six months, and preferably, up to one year is required to conduct a search and selection of a new president.

The search committee will need to establish a timetable for its activities. It should schedule its complex work with time deadlines for each stage in the process. The flow chart on the next page illustrates the various steps. The chart is excerpted from *The Search Process*, published by the American Council on Education in 1973.

A minimum of six months and, preferably, up to one year is required to conduct a search and selection of a new president. A board will want to make its decision approximately six months prior to the designee's actually taking office. Creating the necessary committee structure, developing the description of the position, soliciting nominations and applications, screening candidates and conducting interviews will take at least six months or more.

Fig. 1: THE SEARCH PROCESS*

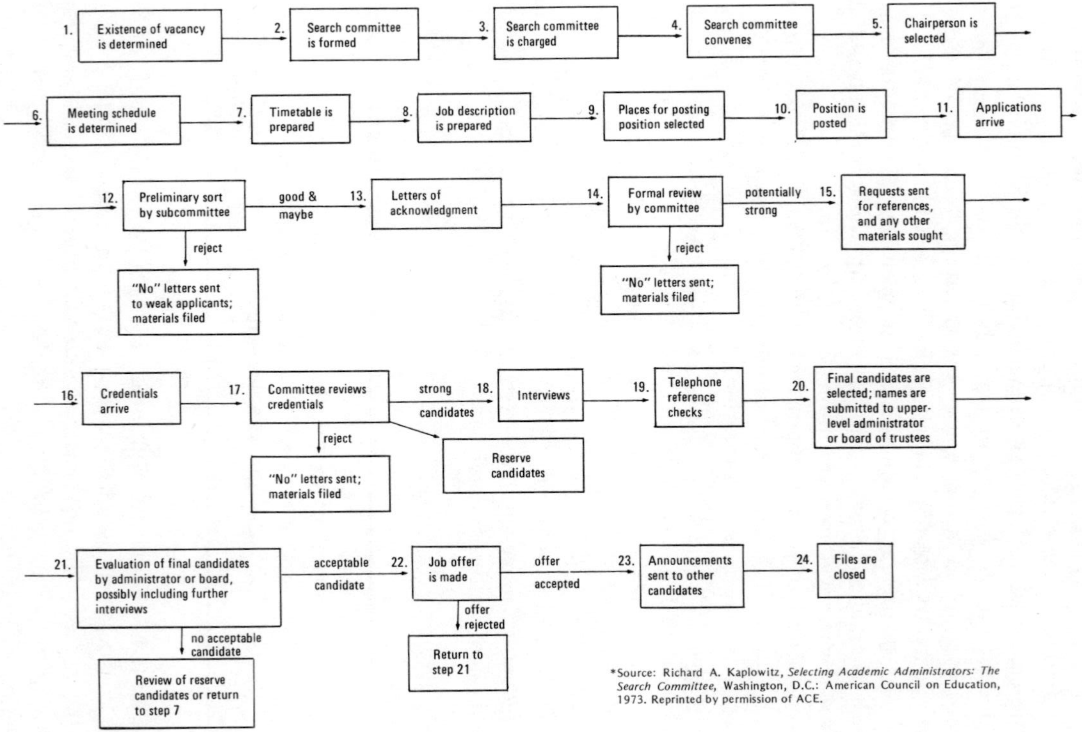

*Source: Richard A. Kaplowitz, *Selecting Academic Administrators: The Search Committee*, Washington, D.C., American Council on Education, 1973. Reprinted by permission of ACE.

The search process requires staff assistance, an office where candidate credentials and other records may be kept with adequate security, and sufficient financial resources for telephone, postage, printing, secretarial assistance and possible travel for interviews and on-site visits. Neither committee members nor candidates should be expected to bear such costs personally.

We shall now deal with the ingredients of the search process itself—establishing the qualifications and criteria for selection, obtaining nominations and applications from candidates and the various screening procedures leading to a small group of finalists for consideration.

QUALIFICATIONS AND CRITERIA

There are various viewpoints and practices in regard to developing a statement of qualifications for a presidential vacancy. Some institutions issue an extensive list of qualifications that could not possibly be met by any living candidate. It would be sheer arrogance for any candidate to declare that he or she possessed such qualifications.*

One favorite quotation is that of the Yale trustee who is alleged to have commented as follows on the election of President Griswold:

> He had to be a leader, a magnificent speaker and great writer, a good public relations man and fund raiser, a man of iron health and stamina, married to a paragon—a combination Queen Victoria, Florence Nightingale, and best dressed woman of the year—a man of the world, but with great spiritual qualities, an experienced administrator who can delegate authority, a Yale man and a great scholar, and a social philosopher who has at his fingertips a solution to all of the world's problems. I don't doubt that you have concluded that there is only One who has most of these qualifications. But, we had to ask ourselves—is God a Yale man?[21]

Manning M. Pattillo urges that the committee should "resist the temptation to prepare a flowery statement on the ideal candidate." He observes that

---

*I have always been fond of the description of the various types of human character described by Aristotle in *The Rhetoric*, Book II. Aristotle portrays the Youthful type of character in words to which most college administrators will give their assent. ("They have exalted notions, because they have not yet been humbled by life. . . .") He also portrays the character of Elderly Men—"past their prime, sure about nothing, under-do everything."

For men in their prime, in between the young and the elderly, "they have neither that excess of confidence which amounts to rashness, nor too much timidity, but the right amount of each. They neither trust everybody nor distrust everybody, but judge people correctly."

Aristotle would have suggested selecting presidents who are "in their prime."

"two qualifications are probably indispensable for any prospective president: successful experience as a senior administrator and commitment to the type of institution he is to head (such as a liberal arts college, or state university or private university)."[22]

Criteria for the selection should be related to the needs of the individual institution. The challenge is to match specific talents, skills, experiences and commitments to one's own institution. Thus, borrowing statements from other colleges does not make much sense. David L. McKenna says

> **Criteria for the selection should be related to the needs of the individual institution. The challenge is to match specific talents, skills, experiences and commitments to one's own institution. Thus, borrowing other college's statements does not make much sense.**

that criteria for selecting presidents should be "situational rather than personal." He advises, "Rather than starting with the personality of the president, the beginning point should be the personality of the institution. . . . A 'situational' appraisal of a college in preparation for a new president also means a precise definition of institutional goals."[23]

Some sample statements of qualifications will be found below:

1. State University of New York: Board of Trustees Standards (1973)

Recognizing that no criteria should be viewed as an absolute requirement, the Trustees nonetheless expect that certain basic qualifications will be taken into account. Among these qualifications are:
- an appropriate background of formal education and evidence of scholarly ability
- substantial successful experience in higher education
- successful administrative experience or promise of administrative ability
- qualities of educational leadership and ability to maintain effective relationships with faculty, students, administrative staff, and others
- evidence or distinct promise of productive community relationships
- age which will both assure a reasonable number of years of educational experience and provide opportunity for a useful period of service before retirement
- personal traits necessary for the most exacting of executive responsibilities, among which are strength of character, intelligence, integrity, humor, fortitude, balance and good judgment, sensitivity to human values, and understanding personality, a capacity for hard work

- good health and physical stamina to meet the pressures of the position

Notwithstanding the foregoing, the Board of Trustees must, of course, reserve the right in its judgment to reject any nominee.

2. University of Arkansas

Presidential Profile (1973)

The University of Arkansas, a multi-campus university system of 22,000 students on six campuses and affiliated units, is seeking a president.

The following characteristics are sought in candidates for the Presidency. A desirable combination of these is expected and candidates will be judged on the basis of overall qualifications.

- Demonstrated scholarly competence including the earned doctorate or its equivalent.
- Successful experience in a college or university setting.
- Significant administrative experience that clearly demonstrates leadership capacity.
- Broad understanding of academic affairs as related to long range planning and implementation.
- Exceptional facility in human relations, including governmental relations.
- Sensitive and broad understanding of the role of the multi-campus state university and its potential for service.
- Knowledge and understanding of the role and function of a land-grant institution.
- Good health, maturity, and vigor.

3. Culver-Stockton College, Canton, Missouri (Private, affiliated with the Christian Church)

What We Are Looking For In Our New President

The president should be a fairly young man, able to give 10 or more years of service to the college. He should be a man of vigor who brings to the leadership of the college a broad cultural view, flexibility of mind, a genuine appreciation for persons and a sense of humor. His personal and professional integrity should be beyond question.

His academic training and experience should have provided him with a knowledge of the aims of church-related liberal arts education and a genuine understanding and respect for the academic community and its role in American democratic society. While an earned doctorate is not a requirement it would be highly desirable for the president to have undergone the academic discipline represented by the doctorate. In addition to his specialized training the president should bring to the position a broad cultural background and an interest in the practical aspects of managing the academic enterprise.

The new president should be knowledgeable about the important place of higher education in the Christian community and the world.

He should be committed to the Judeo-Christian view of life and should have an appreciation of the variety of religious experiences which are appropriately a part of the life of a church-related college. Membership in and knowledge of the life and work of the Christian Church (Disciples of Christ) would be highly desirable in the new president. However, a broad ecumenical Christian orientation to life and active churchmanship in some Christian body is a requirement.

The new president should understand that Culver-Stockton College is committed to teaching and learning. The new president should have a broad and flexible point of view on economic and political matters. He should not be a "captive" of the old or the new. He should have an appreciation of the value and contributions of the free enterprise system and should also be willing for alternative positions to be presented.

As an administrator the new president should be skillful in involving his colleagues, both faculty and students, in a cooperative effort to maintain a rich and stimulating academic and social life in the college community. He should be open to suggestions from faculty and students. He should possess the organizing ability necessary for the development of a clear sense of purpose and movement of the college among its faculty, students, trustees, alumni and friends. Having involved those who are most intimately concerned with the life of the college, he should have the personal strength and clarity of mind to implement changes when they have been approved by the Board of Trustees. Skill in coordinating and communicating the program which evolves is necessary. Proper management of the college will involve delegation of many specific areas of activity; however, the president must have knowledge of and interest in fianancial management, and professional personnel practices with regard to faculty, staff and students.

He should be a person who can present the college to friends and potential friends convincingly. Ability to lead in developing an organized program of activities to produce the necessary financial support for a program of quality education is necessary. Similarly, he must give effective leadership which will result in attracting able students to the College.* (As revised 6/26/72)

4. University of Wisconsin-Oshkosh.

The following list of qualities to be sought in a chancellor was approved by the Search and Screening Committee in April, 1973. They are stated as broad criteria:

1. Evidence of productive scholarship with a breadth of cultural and intellectual interests;

---

*Any college wishing to adapt this statement or the one from Elmhurst College for its own use should avoid wording which precludes women as possible candidates for the presidency.

2. Demonstrated administrative ability;
   3. Commitment to development of a major public university; and
   4. Sensitivity in faculty, student and community relations.
5. Elmhurst College, Illinois, in its presidential search in 1971, set forth the following as "Desirable Qualifications for the President of Elmhurst College."
   1. Membership in the United Church of Christ would not be essential, but deep and sincere Christian conviction is required.
   2. Though not required, "an earned doctoral degree" would add to the candidate's stature. The candidate, whether he be from the business or educational world, should have a sound philosophy of education. An individual's achievements in administration and teaching are of great interest to the nominating committee.
   3. Achievement in fund raising will receive serious consideration by the Presidential Nominating Committee.
   4. The candidate should be an effective speaker because he will represent Elmhurst College to students, faculty, other administrators in the academic and business worlds and to the general public.
   5. The President of Elmhurst College should be an effective administrator who can work well with all types of men and women. He should know how to delegate responsibility and authority, but at the same time he should be strong enough to demand top-quality performance on the part of his staff and faculty. He must be willing and able to make difficult decisions within a consistent overall philosophy and have the courage to follow them through.
   6. The President must be an innovator able to inspire students, faculty and Board of Trustees to help him achieve the goals he envisions as reflecting higher education's changing role in society.
   7. The President should be a person able to relate to all segments of the college and local community and should demonstrate an empathy to the particular concerns of students, alumni, faculty and staff. He should be able to serve in various community leadership positions.
   8. He should be a man who is able to bring philosophic and religious perspectives to bear upon the institution.
   9. He needs to be the kind of person who can relate to the church's changing role in higher education on a local and national level.

OBTAINING NOMINATIONS AND CANDIDATES

There is much conflicting advice as to how extensive an effort should be made to elicit nominations and applications for a presidential opening. Some institutions, because of their circumstances, may seek an internal candidate and thus avoid any external search. Others, because of their local or regional nature, will not profit from a major, national effort to obtain nominations. Most institutions, however, will seek external as well as internal candidates and will want to give fair consideration to the widest possible pool of applicants.

Affirmative Action

With the advent of Affirmative Action/Equal Opportunity requirements, it is clearly inadvisable to restrict any external search to nominees from only a few, restricted sources. Such a limited search may not only violate the spirit and letter of government regulations or legislation, but it can also offend some of the constituencies which the institution serves.

Almost all colleges and universities are covered by provisions of Executive Order 11246, as amended, Title VII of the Civil Rights Act and Title IX of the Education Amendments Act of 1972 (Higher Education Act). Public colleges and universities may also have to be responsive to various state regulations in recruitment and hiring.

Obviously, discrimination is prohibited but legal requirements go beyond that. An institution should be able to provide evidence that, in its recruitment procedures, it has made a meaningful search, attempting to solicit all appropriately qualified applicants, including women and minorities. Thus, resorting merely to "word of mouth" recruiting would be improper.

Many institutions will engage in "affirmative advertising", making clear that women and minorities are welcome to apply and become candidates. In published notices and advertisements, the description of the presidential opening will contain the phrase, "An Equal Opportunity Employer, M/F." The statement of qualifications for the position should describe the criteria to be used in selecting the new president. Such criteria should not be formulated to restrict candidates on the basis of race and sex.

With the new requirements, many colleges and universities will use advertisements to demonstrate the openness of their search. Announcements of presidential vacancies are seen frequently in the Sunday edition of the *New York Times* and, especially, in *The Chronicle of Higher Education.** Such advertisements should solicit both nominations and applications. They should provide a brief description of the institution, qualifications sought for the position, a deadline date for receipt of names and an address for further correspondence.

In addition to advertising, most institutions will want to announce the availability of the position in a variety of other places. Some people overestimate the restrictive nature of affirmative action and equal opportunity requirements. For example, a general announcement or advertisement for a presidential vacancy does not prevent the committee from soliciting nominations and applications from a variety of other sources as well.

---

*For example, the June 24, 1974 issue of *The Chronicle of Higher Education* contained announcements of nine presidential vacancies for which nominations and applications were solicited.

As long as the same criteria and requirements are used to evaluate all candidates, a search which extends beyond those who apply is perfectly appropriate and desirable. This expanded search might well include specific solicitation of sources for women and minority, including minority women, candidates.*

> In reading the published material on the subject of presidential succession, it is startling to note the almost automatic presumption that presidential candidates, finalists and appointees will be male. Governing boards and search committees should make every effort to encourage women to seek to become heads of institutions of higher learning.

In reading the published material on the subject of presidential succession, it is startling to note the almost automatic presumption that presidential candidates, finalists and appointees will be male. Governing boards and search committees should make every effort to encourage women to seek to become heads of institutions of higher learning. Search committees should be aware of and use available resources to identify qualified female candidates. Among the sources for such candidates are the following:

1. Higher Education Referral Services, Brown University, Box 1901, Providence, Rhode Island 02912. (This center, funded by the Ford Foundation, serves as a national clearinghouse for faculty and administrative openings for women.)
2. Cooperative College Registry, One Dupont Circle, N.W., Suite 10, Washington, D.C. 20036.
3. National Council of Administrative Women in Education, 1815 E. Fort Myer Drive, N. Arlington, Virginia 22209.

EXPANDING THE SEARCH FOR CANDIDATES

In addition to the possibility of placing an advertisement or public announcement of the position in various national publications, committees will want to seek nominations from a wide variety of sources. These would include news releases to various associations in the field of higher education, making known the opening and the procedure to be followed if interested

---

*The Project on the Status and Education of Women of the Association of American Colleges can provide a list of women's caucuses within the learned societies and other recruiting resources.

persons wish to communicate with the search committee.* They would also include announcements to the faculty, alumni, students and other constituencies of the institution.

Some institutions communicate with a large number of college and university presidents, foundation and educational association executives, indicating their interest in receiving nominations of qualified persons whom they can consider. Committees should feel free to follow-up with these nominees, by inquiring whether they are willing to be considered for the post, without an implied commitment on the part of either party.

Although persons experienced in public higher education are getting used to the "goldfish bowl" nature of their existence, it is still true that many persons are reluctant to place themselves in the position of *applicant* for such an office. This is especially true for persons who already occupy a presidency. Few persons in such a position want to commit themselves to leaving their present post but may be willing to consider a possible job change. In the private sector, and particularly in many church-related colleges, aspirants to the presidency may believe that they must be "called" to the office. It is not unusual in some private institutions for search committees to compile lists of nominees, sort and screen them, without informing the persons involved. In some large multi-campus public systems, a senior administrative officer is assigned the task of developing and maintaining lists of highly qualified prospects to be considered when vacancies occur. For example, the Regents of the University of California have a formally approved statement of procedures to be followed in the appointment of campus chancellors which provides that: "The President of the University will conduct a continuous search for promising candidates for chancellorships. This will obviate the necessity for a systematic, nationwide search each time a vacancy occurs."

It is recommended that initial announcements and communications to applicants and nominees make clear that only an expression of interest and a resumé are sought. Standard biographical information is all that is required at the outset, and it is inappropriate to ask for letters of reference and other materials before they are needed.

If a search committee wishes to approach or encourage presidents of other colleges and universities to consider becoming candidates, they should avoid placing them in the position of "applicant" or "candidate" prematurely. A president may be willing to be "considered" but wish to avoid the appearance of job-hunting. Only after an institution reaches the latter stages of the search should these "invited" candidates be required to decide whether they wish to proceed with personal interviews and the checking of references.

---

*The various associations of colleges and universities are often a good source for nominations. These associations include: Association of American Colleges, American Council on Education, Association of American Universities, American Association of State Colleges and Universities, National Association of State Universities and Land-Grant Colleges, and American Association of Community and Junior Colleges.

For a variety of reasons, fair and equitable treatment does not require rigid adherence to a single procedure for the identification and initial screening of candidates. A variety of methods may all meet the test of fairness.

At the outset, every effort should be made to introduce into the system some clear understanding of the ground rules concerning confidentiality. These should be known to the committee members and the candidates.

Many of the persons being considered for the vacancy will be concerned with the search committee's treatment of their correspondence and information gathered from references. At the outset, every effort should be made to achieve a clear understanding of the ground rules concerning confidentiality. These should be known to the committee members and the candidates. The ground rules may need to be different at various stages of the search process, especially in those public institutions where state legislation may effect the conduct of the committee. Most certainly, all members of a search committee should be expected to regard all deliberations of the committee as confidential. Public statements about the progress of the committee should be made only by its chairperson.

SCREENING AND ASSESSING THE CANDIDATES

Initial Screening

The initial screening of nominees and applicants should have as its purpose the elimination of persons who obviously do not meet the basic qualifications that have been set. The committee should not start this task until final agreement on qualifications has been reached. If the criteria are clear it will not be necessary for all members of the screening group to read each resumé in the initial screening. However, some record should be kept of the basic reason(s) why an applicant is eliminated at this initial stage of the screening process.* The chairperson of the committee should notify such persons of their elimination from consideration at the conclusion of this first stage.

If a large group of candidates survive the initial screening, it may be desirable to reduce the number further by full committee study of creden-

---

*Careful records should be kept of all actions of the committee, in each stage of the process. Such record-keeping not only encourages a more systematic screening and evaluation of candidates but may be required in the defense of any challenge to the fairness of the committee's actions.

tials, before requesting additional data. After the initial screening the committee should communicate in writing with those candidates still under consideration. This communication should include a request for confirmation of a continuing interest in the position and additional data that may be required, including references and permission to contact them.

Additional evidence of motivation or commitment may be requested at this stage. For example, one independent liberal arts college asked those who survived the initial screening to provide a written statement expressing the candidate's personal views on the place of the liberal arts in higher education and the future of private liberal arts colleges. The successful candidate in that search made the following observations on that request. "Looking back, I am sure that I did my share of grumbling. In retrospect, however, this proved to be an important part of the process. In addition to the statement on philosophy and questions of future expectations, it provided an opportunity to see how well the candidate expressed himself in writing. Communication is always a difficult task for a college president. An unintentional 'tone' can be devastating."

References

Some screening committees ask the candidate to have letters of reference sent directly to the committee. Others merely request names of persons to be contacted by the committee in writing or by telephone. Sometimes the reference check is open-ended in nature. Other committees prefer a highly structured evaluation form which may even involve some kind of quantitative rating scheme. When seeking references, it is advisable to describe the nature of the institution and to inform the referee of the criteria which have been established for the position. This procedure will help the respondent focus his or her evaluation on matters of direct concern to the committee. Otherwise, most letters of reference will be positive but extremely general in nature. Some responses will require follow-up telephone calls to clarify or expand upon items of concern to the committee.

The essential purpose of this stage of the evaluation process is to reduce the list of candidates to a reasonable number of highly qualified persons to be interviewed personally, visited, and evaluated further. If the committee is expected to present a list of three to five finalists to the board, or its selection committee, it will need to reduce the pool of candidates at this stage to no more than 15 or 20. Again, a written record should be kept of evaluative decisions. Candidates eliminated from further consideration should receive notification.

Interviews

Individual institutions or systems structure the selection process in accordance with their own needs and characteristics. Several different approaches to the interview process are described below. If a *single* all-college committee has authority to search, screen and make the selection, candidates may only be required to make a single campus visit. Other institutions will have more complex procedures which may involve advisory groups, screening committees, and other campus and community groups in the interview process. In such cases, the goal of preliminary interviews should be to identify three to five final candidates to be recommended to the committee making the actual selection. That group, in turn, will wish to conduct additional interviews with finalists and their spouses, and may also want to conduct their own background investigations.

When advisory groups are involved, the selection committee must develop a procedure for receiving adequate and accurate summaries of their evaluations of candidates. A form or statement of the criteria and qualifications for the position, with space for evaluative comments or ratings, is a useful device in such circumstances.

In many public institutions, and some larger private ones, it is not uncommon for semi-finalist candidates to be subjected to what have been called "marathon" interviews. In the "marathon" situation, candidates are interviewed not only by the search and screening committee but are also made available to various constituent groups in the institution—faculty, staff, students, alumni and community. If such a procedure is to be used, candidates should be told in advance. Obviously, such a procedure precludes the possibility of confidentiality. Anyone who agrees to engage in such a lengthy, and often aggressive, process must be strongly motivated to seek the presidency. At this point, competition between qualified candidates may develop and representatives of various constituencies will become interested in the views, positions, manner and personalities of the various "contestants." Some people are offended by the very idea of "marathon" interview sessions, which may involve a candidate for a full two-day period. Others defend the practice on the grounds that it is a realistic approximation of roles a president must play in a complex institution.

There is a necessary tension in the entire search, screening and selection procedure: between (1) a process that would be gentle and attractive to excellent candidates, and (2) a more open process that enables a microcosm of the institution to participate in order to achieve an initial consensus of all the groups who might otherwise attempt to withhold legitimization of the new leader. In the gentle process, candidates may be given a very distorted view of the realities of the post. On the other hand, some candidates will not want to subject themselves to the open process for fear they may be rejected or that it may not bring out their best qualities. Each institution will have to deal with these tensions and decide for itself how to arrange the process. Either way, there are advantages and disadvantages.

Whether the process is open or closed, candidates will be asked to express their views on a wide variety of matters. Board members and faculty will be concerned with academic governance, educational philosophy, faculty authority, collective bargaining, tenure, management of financial resources, fund-raising, athletics and the like. Students may press the candidates for their views on speaker policy, parietal rules, drugs, homosexuality, alcohol

---

There is a necessary tension in the entire search, screening and selection procedure: between (1) a process that would be gentle and attractive to excellent candidates, and (2) a more open process that enables a microcosm of the institution to participate in order to achieve an initial consensus of all the groups who might otherwise attempt to withhold legitimization of the new leader.

---

and student evaluation of faculty. In addition, representatives of women's and minority groups will ask searching questions concerning a candidate's attitude and willingness to take a stand on controversial matters about which the campus community itself may be divided.

When this process has yielded from three to five persons, all of whom are considered qualified and fully acceptable to the search and screening group, these names will be reported to those empowered to select the president.

Making the Final Decision

The selection group must now choose the new president. It has before it a short list of candidates who have survived a very rigorous screening process. Biographical data, assessments from references and the observations of advisory groups are at hand.

But the sorting process is a two-way street. Some candidates may have been discouraged or dismayed by what they have learned about an institution and its problems. Others will have been reinforced in their desire to become its president. All should have a fairly good idea of the institution's problems and prospects. Those candidates who have survived the screening process to this point, and still seek the position, should be treated with the utmost personal consideration, for the final stage is one of great delicacy. Desirable candidates may withdraw if they are not treated properly by the committee or by board members. The top persons on the list may need to be sold on the opportunity of this particular presidency.

> **But the sorting process is a two-way street. Some candidates may have been discouraged or dismayed by what they have have learned about an institution and its problems. Others will have been reinforced in their desire to become its president. All should have a fairly good idea of the institution's problems and prospects. Those candidates who have survived the screening process to this point, and still seek the position, should be treated with the utmost personal consideration, for the final stage can be one of great delicacy. Desirable candidates may withdraw if they are not treated properly by the committee or by board members. The top persons on the list may need to be sold on the opportunity of this particular presidency.**

PERSONAL INQUIRIES OF ASSOCIATES

The selection group will want to make discreet inquiries about the final candidates from associates and others with whom they have had working relationships. In many cases the board chairperson will want to participate actively in the selection process at this stage. In multi-campus systems, the head of the system will now become directly involved.

A common practice is for "on-site" visits to take place prior to the final interviews. This entails sending representatives of the selection group to the present location of the candidate to assess relationships, reputation and the regard in which he or she is held. Such visits should definitely be cleared with each candidate and should not be a surprise.

On-site visits are controversial and have disadvantages as well as advantages. Each institution will have to decide for itself the efficacy of the practice. These visits enable representatives of the selection committee to talk to the candidate's professional colleagues, board members and appropriate community leaders. During a visit one gains impressions that might not otherwise be gleaned from letters, references or the initial interview. A visit may reveal issues, personality traits, and strengths or weaknesses which will need to be explored in the final interviews.

Yet it should also be remembered that any one of the final candidates may be the desired choice for president. The development of a sound working relationship begins during the selection process. Some candidates may resent an on-site visit, especially if it appears to focus only on negative aspects of past performance. Committee members who participate in such visits should strive for balance as they pursue their inquiry.

One successful candidate, recently appointed to the presidency of a private university, had this to say about on-site interviews.

> My major reservation about a trip made to the candidate's home campus is that it is an uncomfortable experience that is not very productive. It has a tendency to emphasize a negative evaluation on the part of the candidate in regard to his present role. There is no turning back at this point and thus it is a rather one-sided proposition. I do believe there are better ways in which one can verify the letters of reference and other information than to make an on-site call. It was at this point that I felt I was a ripe apple being possibly picked or sold.

FINAL INTERVIEWS

The final interview between the candidate and those who will make the actual selection should be a matter of careful preparation on the part of the selecting group and the finalist candidates.

The board should assume the full expenses of each candidate and spouse. The attitude of the spouse is very important and will influence the candidate's decision. Thoughtful treatment by the board will signal their appropriate awareness of family needs. If there are small children in the candidate's family, an offer of reimbursement for child-care during the parents' absence should also be made. Arrangements should be made for the candidate's spouse to see the campus, the presidential residence if there is one, and the local community.

Those conducting the final interview should know what ground they wish to cover and be prepared to indicate their own views regarding problems, priorities and objectives for the institution. They should provide various types of helpful information, including budgets and financial reports. They should also be prepared to answer the candidate's searching questions.

For the candidate, this may be the last opportunity to obtain information vital to a decision for acceptance if the presidency is offered. Before the interview, or during the campus visit, a candidate should ask to see the agendas and minutes of past governing board meetings, minutes of faculty meetings for the previous year, a copy of the personnel policies covering faculty, copies of student newspapers, campus newsletters and other relevant materials. Every effort should be made for a full exchange of information.

> **Those conducting the final interview should know what ground they wish to cover and be prepared to indicate their own views regarding problems, priorities and objectives for the institution. They should provide various types of helpful information, including budgets and financial reports. They should also be prepared to answer the candidate's searching questions.**

The final interview provides a last opportunity for the selection group and the candidate to "size up" one another. It should also clarify the nature of the expected relationship between the president and the board and provide a complete appraisal of priorities, problems and the institution's finances. The interview procedure should provide an opportunity if desired for the candidate to meet individually with the board chairperson or key committee chairpersons.

Recently, J. Stephen Collins surveyed the opinions of a sample of college presidents who had left office over the past five years. He reports that forty-five percent of the respondents said, in retrospect, that in the selection process they had gone through, the board did not have a clear understanding of its own duties and responsibilities. Sixty percent said that their boards did not have a clear understanding of plans or goals for their institution for the succeeding 5 to 10 years.[24]

In the same study, former presidents were asked to identify those major items of information a candidate should have before deciding to accept a presidency. The two most frequent responses were: (1) substantial knowledge about the financial status of the institution and, (2) more knowledge of the Board itself and a clear understanding of its expectations.

By the end of the interview process, the selection group should have identified one or several persons it is willing to recommend to the appointing authority for the presidency. The committee may wish to rank several candidates in order so that if negotiations with the first choice prove unsuccessful, it can proceed to the next without question.

It should be clear to the entire college community that if the process to this point has not yielded a satisfactory candidate the search and screening group can be asked to provide additional names.

Making the Appointment

> *"Remember that you are asking the new president to take a very demanding position, one of the most demanding in American life. Therefore, provide him with an attractive salary and perquisites and see that he has the strong backing of the board. As with anyone else, he needs friendship, cooperation, and thoughtful counsel to do his best work, and the provision of these necessities is one of the most important duties of the trustees."*[25]

Once the board has made its choice, the actual terms of the appointment must be arranged. The chairperson of the board or a subcommittee of the board should meet with the candidate chosen to negotiate the actual agreement. Depending upon the nature of the previous discussions, this is the time for all terms, conditions and expectations to be resolved to the mutual satisfaction of the chosen candidate and the governing board, before any announcement is made. Until these negotiations are satisfactorily completed the remaining candidates should not be informed of the board's decision. If agreement cannot be reached with the favored candidate or the invitation to serve as president is declined it may be necessary to move on down the list of finalists.

Frederick deW. Bolman has advised governing boards, in concluding final negotiations, to make what has been called "The Harvard Offer."[26] Before formally electing the chosen candidate to the presidency, the governing board inquires of the candidate, "If, on the basis of our negotiated understandings, you are invited to be our president, will you accept?" This procedure may save embarrassment for both parties.

All agreements reached and the actual terms of the apointment should be put into writing.

The governing board should know, before negotiations begin, what terms it is willing to offer, including the salary, fringe benefits, conditions and understandings it wishes to establish. It should be made clear to the candidate that agreement on these issues is a prerequisite to formal completion of the appointment.

Similarly, the candidate should have a clear notion of his or her expectations. It is at this point that some finalist candidates, flattered by the outcome of the search, may feel that it is crass or inappropriate to review such matters before saying "yes" to the offer of appointment. This can only lead to future conflict over the differing perceptions and expectations that may have seemed implicit to one side or the other in the agreement.

One recently appointed president of a private college, expressed his thoughts on this subject retrospectively, "Regarding job conditions, I think it would be a good idea if the search committee, or the trustees, in the final interview, had a list of the items that should be included. Apparently, because many of these areas are considered 'negotiable', the committee may assume that the candidate will bring them up. If the candidate fails to mention any of these items, then the standard policies that the board of trustees has in mind may not be consistent with the candidate's view."

SUBJECTS TO COVER

The first items on the agenda for negotiation will be the obvious ones of salary, fringe benefits, moving expenses, starting date and the like. Retirement plan provisions ought to be clarified, including the transferability of the candidate's present retirement plan, and the amount of employer contribution.

Contract

Some colleges and universities will want to consider some form of term appointment or contract, although it should be *unmistakably clear that the president serves at the pleasure of the governing board*. Nevertheless, some type of provision for terminal leave or separation pay is in order whether or not a specified term of appointment is set.

Some public systems of higher education have established term appointments or contracts which guarantee certain employment rights to presidents, including academic rank and tenure. Most have not, however, and no particular trend has developed in this direction. The State University of New York System and The Minnesota State College System are among those offering term appointments.

Some colleges and universities will want to consider some form of term appointment or contract, although it should be <u>unmistakably clear that the president serves at the pleasure of the governing board</u>. Nevertheless, some type of provision for terminal leave or separation pay is in order whether or not a specified term of appointment is set.

The Board of Trustees of the multi-campus State University of New York approved in 1973 an appointment policy which provides the following:

> ... *shall serve for a period of five years, during which period the appointee shall serve at the pleasure of the Board of Trustees. ... Unless reappointed, the service of a chief administrative officer shall terminate at the conclusion of an appointive*

period. Prior to the expiration of any appointive period the Board of Trustees may formally evaluate the services of the chief administrative officer and may reappoint the incumbent to serve at the pleasure of the Board for a subsequent five year period.

A chief administrative officer, upon appointment, shall be appointed by the Chancellor to the faculty of the University in a position of academic rank with continuing appointment.

Louis H. Heilbron, former Chairman of the Board of Trustees of the California State University and Colleges System offers a different view. He believes the campus presidents should serve without any fixed term. On the matter of contracts, he states:

A contract term is usually not stipulated. It is better for the institution and for its leader to have freedom in this respect. If the chief executive loses control of the institution, or if he finds that he is unable to work with the board, an unexpired contract period will only be an obstacle to the inevitable and necessary dissolution. The attitude of most presidents is, if they don't want me, I no longer want them.[27]

Whatever the board's policy on this matter, terms of employment and other agreements should be clarified fully before the appointment is completed.

President's House

Most colleges and universities provide either a residence on or near the campus, or some form of housing allowance to enable their president to host various functions on behalf of the institution. It is important to clarify the matter of housing, for it can become a major burden for new presidents unaware of its significance.

If the president's house is located on campus there may be little privacy for the president's family. If the house is regarded as a college facility, where various social events are scheduled, that makes for a very different kind of situation than if it is defined as the president's domicile. If the latter, then president and spouse can exercise some control over the use of the house and its availability to college and community groups.

If the president's house will be used for entertainment and a variety of social functions for members of the governing board, faculty, students, alumni and donors, then it becomes vital to have a clear understanding concerning the extent to which the college or the president is responsible for refurnishing, decorating, maintaining and supporting the facility and funding such functions. Is the president responsible for such expenses or does the institution provide such support? Many presidents have learned, to their sorrow, that trying to meet the hosting expectations of a governing board has led to criticism and controversy, if not within the president's family, then perhaps within the faculty or community.

> **A large, spacious president's house may appear to be a "fringe-benefit" to a governing board, but it can also be a major burden and millstone to a president if it is not properly maintained and supported.**

Household help should also be a matter that is settled at this point. Although most presidents are married, it should not be presumed by the board that the presence of a spouse means the presence of an unpaid housekeeper and cook for official entertainment functions. Whether the prsident is married or unmarried, the president's house should have appropriate household help commensurate with the expectations of the board and the college community regarding its use in the overall college program and environment. A large, spacious president's house may appear to be a "fringe-benefit" to a governing board, but it can also be a major burden and millstone to a president if it is not properly maintained and supported.

President's Spouse

There was a time when it was presumed that, with few exceptions, the president would be a man and a married one at that. Almost all of the writing on the presidency makes such an assumption and refers to the president not only with the pronoun "he," but with numerous references to his "wife." Elsewhere in this publication search and selection committees are urged to make earnest efforts to encourage the nomination and candidacy of qualified women be they married or single. Even so, the fact is that most college presidents today are men who are married. Therefore, the wife of a president may be expected by the board to assume significant responsibilities related to her husband's position. Because of changing social attitudes, the expected role of the president's spouse may be an especially sensitive area of concern.

The spouse plays an important part in the successful performance of a married president. Very often the selection committee's reactions to the spouse will be crucial to the final decision. Expectations regarding the role of the spouse should not be taken for granted. If the leading candidate is a man, the board's expectations of his wife should be explicit and not left unspoken. Is the wife expected to be a "partner" in the enterprise or is she able to have her own career if that is her choice? What are her obligations as an official hostess? What arrangements are made for entertainment, travel and child-care expenses? What secretarial and housekeeping assistance will be available?

Muriel Beadle, wife of the former president of the University of Chicago, offers her own thoughts after returning home with her husband from a presidential interview:

> *For my part, the idea of running that house was appalling. A thousand faculty wives to get to know. Eight thousand students. Goodness knows what other responsibilities. At Caltech, I had observed Doris DuBridge's activities with sympathy, and I doubted that I could be as consistently nice as she was to people I didn't like very much. Given my inability to dissemble, I'd surely lose the University some multimillion-dollar gift by insulting a potential donor. I am an activist; could I restrict myself to non-controversial kinds of activism? And I detest cocktail parties. What the University of Chicago needed, I was thinking as we flew back to California that night, was a First Lady who had more social savvy than I had.*[28]

For the most part, governing boards have not given appropriate consideration to the wife of a president. With changing attitudes and younger presidents, boards will have to face new realities concerning the automatic presumption that the wife will preside as official hostess. She should be granted the right of a separate career if that is her choice.

When it is clear that the president's wife is willing to play the part of a working team member, the institution should make adequate provisions to aid her in doing so.* When the president is required to travel extensively,

---

> **For the most part, governing boards have not given appropriate consideration to the wife of a president. With changing attitudes and younger presidents, boards will have to face new realities concerning the automatic presumption that the wife will preside as official hostess. She should be granted the right of a separate career if that is her choice.**

---

*Institutions may be limiting themselves seriously in candidate selection if they insist on the wife being an unpaid part of the presidential team without an opportunity for her own career. It is the writer's view that more younger couples will seek to avoid such a requirement as unduly restrictive.

Times are changing rapidly in this area. It was only in 1969 that the job description for the presidency of a prestigious private college in the Midwest contained the following description:

> "Marital status: candidate should be married—the President's wife is an important part of the team. She must be energetic, personable; capable of being an excellent hostess to all the groups that make up the college's publics—students, faculty, trustees, alumni, distinguished visitors, etc. Wives of all candidates being seriously considered must be interviewed."

representing the institution at alumni gatherings, with potential donors, or at national conferences, it should be assumed that the institution will pay for the travel expenses of the wife as well as the president. Concern for the president's family, its lack of privacy, the pressures upon it, the need to get away from the spotlight focused upon it—these are matters to which a board must be sensitive, generous and supportive.

RELATIONSHIPS WITH BOARD

Another area of primary concern is the in-coming president's authority and relationship with the governing board. If the new president is expected to innovate, correct deficiencies and make changes in the institution, will the board recognize and support the personnel changes that may be required to achieve those goals? Are there any "sacred cows" of which the candidates must be made aware? Does the board understand and accept the new president's need for adequate staff support?

> **If the new president is expected to innovate, correct deficiencies and make changes in the institution, will the board recognize and support the personnel changes that may be required to achieve those goals?**

Opportunity should be provided to clarify these understandings and all reporting relationships. A president cannot be effective unless the governing board insists upon appropriate reporting procedures and resists "ends runs" around duly constituted authority. The governing board should give the president ample opportunity to respond to complaints and grievances and not raise such matters initially at board meetings, placing the president in the role of "defendant."

There should also be clarification of the president's external role. Board expectations concerning the extent of the president's activity with the legislature, potential donors, alumni, the community and church relationships ought to be made clear at the outset. If the governing board has strong feelings about such matters as endowment investment policy, fund-raising or relations with the governor, they should be discussed and agreement reached before the new president is appointed. Similarly, any conflicting attitudes concerning the president's personal, political or social activity, business interests, religious affiliation or other matters should be discussed and resolved.

CRITERIA FOR EVALUATION

Most presidential appointment processes do not deal adequately with evaluation procedures. Nor do they clearly specify the criteria by which the president's effectiveness will be evaluated. If it is mentioned at all, it is an afterthought. After the "honeymoon" period, the president may be criticized for failure to meet objectives that were never mentioned at the time of selection. If a board appoints a new president with the understanding that the budget will be reduced by 15%, it would be grossly unfair to then hold the president responsible for the animosity among the staff which will surely ensue.

In any complex institution there is plenty that can go wrong. Since the president is the one person directly responsible to the governing board, the president is often the focus of all criticism—be it related to student conduct, faculty salary demands or the economic condition of the institution. In a sense, the president must accept these responsibilities. But presidential evaluation should focus on performance related to the goals or criteria set forth at the time of appointment.

David L. McKenna recommends that "performance goals" ought to be agreed upon at the time of the president's selection. He suggests that a three-to-five year evaluation should be planned to assess a president's effectiveness.

> *Once the performance goals for the man and the institution have been defined, evaluation is a natural process. As it is now, presidents may have contracts or agreements, but they serve at the pleasure of the board. Under this system, presidential evaluation is a whimsical and emotional process which swings from character investigations to sentimental testimonials. Performance goals and planned evaluations will put some stability into the system and take some emotion out of the process. Rather than evaluating a president by likes and dislikes, his effectiveness should be measured by the degree to which he has met the performance goals which were agreed upon at the time of his selection.*[29]

Not all institutions are prepared to state "performance goals" at the outset. Many governing boards desperately search for a new president precisely because they require help in defining the goals and objectives of their institution and need someone to guide their own activity. Nevertheless, some effort should be made to provide a president with constructive feedback and periodic counseling. There should be a sharing of a board's concerns and a willingness to provide the assistance necessary to overcome difficulties. Warren Bennis noted that the presidential search can become a "search and destroy" mission. Every effort must be made to help the new president succeed. It will be tragic if a board, even unwittingly, contributes to the destruction of a president it has searched so hard to find.

A number of institutions, both public and private, have introduced evaluation procedures in recent years. Some were initiated by governing boards of public systems of higher education while others, primarily in the private sector, were established at the request of presidents.

In 1973, the State University of New York adopted a policy of five-year term appointments coupled with a formal evaluation procedure for those presidents who seek reappointment. The guidelines for that evaluation clearly state that the process of presidential review is entirely different from the process of selection and that presidential review is clearly a function of the trustees.

The criteria against which the president's effectiveness is reviewed are those defined responsibilities and basic qualifications which were taken into account in the search process. In addition to the president's own prepared statement of self-assessment, an *ad hoc* evaluation committee prepares a written appraisal, evaluating the president's performance in respect to:

1. Academic leadership and management
2. Administrative leadership and management
3. The institutional tone set by the president
4. Internal relationships
5. External relationships
6. Sensitivity to the needs of campus

The Oregon State System of Higher Education has been exploring the possibility of adopting specific criteria for evaluating the performance of campus presidents. Although no formal action to adopt specific criteria has yet been taken, the Board of Higher Education has been considering the following "suggested criteria":

1. Physical condition
2. Energy
3. Administrative competence
4. Relationships with Board's office
5. Relationships with other institutions
6. Relationships with institution staff and students
7. Relationships with State government
   a) Executive Department
   b) Legislature
   c) Other
8. Relationships with public, especially the local public

In 1973 the Minnesota State College System adopted a new policy for its presidents which included a five-year term appointment. Under this policy, each president will be evaluated during the third year of office and, again in the fifth year. The specific criteria to be utilized in the evaluation have not yet been approved but the process includes the use of outside consultants to assist in the assessment of performance. Following evaluation the president may be asked to serve a new term or be offered a faculty position.

Private colleges and universities have also developed evaluation procedures. Best known, perhaps, is the action of President Kingman Brewster, who called for an appraisal of his leadership at Yale in 1970, as a condition for continuing in office beyond a seventh year.

In 1972, President John Coleman requested the Haverford College Board of Managers to make a thorough study of his past performance and future promise. The Board appointed a Presidential Evaluation Committee which conducted an extensive survey involving faculty, staff, students and alumni.

The criteria for the evaluation of President Coleman's performance were expressed in the form of "evaluative benchmarks." These were:

1. Administrative ability
2. Relations with various segments of the Haverford community
3. Personal qualities—objectivity, fairness, humanness, sensitivity, honesty, openness
4. Commitment to scholarship and academic excellence
5. Commitment to Quaker values—moral dimensions
6. Commitment to Haverford College as an institution
7. Quality of leadership and decision-making ability

A lengthy and candid evaluative report was written, identifying strengths and weaknesses. After examining the President's performance in terms of the "benchmarks," the Committee recommended that John Coleman be invited to continue his service to Haverford College as its President.

Recently, Alfred University conducted an evaluation of its president pursuant to its policy to do so every four years. The evaluation committee consisted of three trustees, with backgrounds in administration. a representative cross-section of the Alfred University community was interviewed, including faculty, staff, students and parents.

The Alfred University Committee addressed itself to these principal questions:

1. How is the president regarded by the university community?
2. How well is the administrative system functioning?
3. How can some of the burdens of the office be lightened to permit more time for fund-raising?
4. Are the president's salary and fringe benefits fair and appropriate?

President Leland Miles was continued in office.

This discussion of formal evaluation is not intended to prescribe any particular method of evaluation or set of criteria. One thing is certain—all presidents will be evaluated! Governing boards, faculty, staff, students, alumni and others, will react to the performance of the president and the state of the college or university he or she heads.

Perhaps the examples of formal evaluation procedures described in the preceding paragraphs indicate an attempt toward a more rational procedure than now exists. They are mentioned because assessments of presidential performance need to be thought about and discussed at the time of appointment.

Some presidents will oppose any predetermined time period for evaluation of their performance. Certainly there are disadvantages, as well as advantages, to any formal system which does not take into account the extenuating circumstances that may exist at a prescribed time. Yet sound management and good human relations require some mutual understanding of expectations and ground rules for assessing performance.

CAREER DEVELOPMENT CONCERNS OF PRESIDENTS

Among the concerns of chosen candidates, veteran presidents and enlightened governing boards are those matters which come under the heading of "career development." This is often referred to as "the care and feeding" of presidents.

As we have mentioned earlier, most new presidents attain the office while in their forties and have from 15 to 25 working years ahead of them before normal retirement. As Cohen and March have pointed out in their study of the presidency, "Part of the reason that presidents leave the presidency at a relatively rapid rate around age 50 is that they reach *the age of last opportunity*, after which the quality of jobs for which they qualify starts to deteriorate rapidly."[30]

Given the substantial investment a governing board makes in finding a president, it is simply good management for the board to conserve this important resource. Leadership is a scarce and precious asset that should not be taken for granted.

David L. McKenna talks about "recycling presidents." By the third or fourth year, some presidents grow weary. They have used up most of their energy reserves, as well as quotations and ideas from former reading, and even the best storehouse of dinner-speech jokes has been exhausted. Normal vacations, cut-off from all office communication, are impossible for most. The alternative is often to seek some type of administrative leave for a period of re-creation, or to think about changing jobs before it is too late to do so.

Given the substantial investment a governing board makes in finding a president, it is simply good management for the board to conserve this important resource. Leadership is a scarce and precious asset that should not be taken for granted.

The Association of American Colleges adopted a "Statement on Administrative Leaves" in 1971. The statement suggests that just as a sound program of faculty leaves was of vital importance both to the teacher-scholar and the institution, similar benefits would result from a parallel program of *administrative* leaves. The AAC statement provides this rationale for its proposed policy:

> *The Association particularly recommends that boards of trustees take special steps to provide a regular leave program for the chief administrative officers of our colleges and universities. The purpose and principal benefit of a presidential leave program is to help assure the institution of the highest possible quality of academic leadership. Colleges and universities expend a great deal of effort to identify and secure presidents with sensitivity, imagination and perspective, and are well advised to provide them with opportunities for maintaining those qualities.*
>
> *Personal refreshment and renewal are vital to the maintenance of effective leadership. The unprecedented physical demands and psychological pressures of the college presidency add an element of urgency to the need for administrative leaves. As never before, the unrelenting demands of his office deprive the college president of an opportunity for a normal private life. He, his wife, and often his family, become public figures who must devote unreasonable portions of their time and energy to the welfare of the institution they serve. A presidential leave provides a much needed opportunity for study, relaxation, refreshment and renewal.*
>
> *Presidents, like other administrators and faculty members, may on occasion request leave for a variety of purposes such as public service or the recovery of health. Such requests should be granted whenever suitable arrangements can be made.*

Because of the necessity of careful planning to implement such a policy, the AAC statement also suggests the following procedures:

> *Because of the unique position of the president and the special planning required for implementation of a presidential leave, the governing board of the institution should assume responsibility for initiating this leave program and provide special funding to support it.*
>
> *The president should not be required to "apply" for leave. Instead, the governing board should take the initiative in expressing clearly to the president and the campus community its*

expectation that regular and extended periods away from the day-to-day management of the institution will enhance the president's effectiveness and provide him with the opportunity he needs to gain perspective and to contemplate the future development of the institution.

Although flexibility in scheduling will be necessary, the opportunity for leave should occur regularly and with reasonable frequency, perhaps every three to five years. A president's initial period of leave should not be deferred beyond the fifth year of his tenure in office.

Leaves will vary in length depending upon institutional needs and the president's wishes. Two months is probably the minimum time required to provide a substantial break from administrative duties. Few institutions can afford to be without their president for more than a year.

Since a long presidential absence necessitates careful planning and reassignment of administrative responsibilities, these arrangements should be made well in advance and communicated clearly to the administrative staff and the campus community.

Institutional support of a leave designed to enhance administrative effectiveness clearly implies that the recipient of the leave is expected to return to the institution. Plans, procedures, and authority for his emergency recall during the leave should also be established.[31]

Presenting the New President

The search and selection process is nearly complete. An important phase of an effective conclusion involves the thoughtful announcement of the board's choice and presentation of the new president to the college community and to the public. Release of information to the press and other public relations activities related to the appointment should be carefully planned and well coordinated.

Some public institutions will notify the governor, or other state officials before any public announcement is made. As a courtesy, the search committee, faculty senate officers and representatives of other constituencies can be notified immediately prior to the public announcement.

It is wise to time the public announcement so that it is made with appropriate dignity, rather than appearing as a news leak hastily followed by official confirmation. The other finalist candidates should also be notified that the appointment has been made before the public announcement of the selection.

Whatever the scale of the ceremony, it is important that the leadership selection process conclude with the formal conferring of legitimacy and sanctioned authority on the new president.

The question of presidential inaugurations will, of course, be dealt with in accordance with the unique character of each institution. For some colleges and universities, a major inauguration provides an opportunity to bring all of the respective constituencies together in a ceremony of significance to the entire campus community. For others a modest marking of the occasion may be appropriate. Whatever the scale of the ceremony, it is important that the leadership selection process conclude with the formal conferring of legitimacy and sanctioned authority on the new president.

Epilogue

What has been described here is general and not prescriptive. Each college or university should develop the search, screening and selection procedures that best meet its individual needs. Many will be surprised with the growing openness of selection procedures and the extent to which representatives of the faculty, students, alumni and the campus community may become involved. Despite the clear final authority of the governing board to select and appoint the new president, the trend is clearly toward greater participation in the process by these interested parties.

> **The leadership succession process — sometimes prolonged and irritating to those who must conduct it — is calculated to heighten the possibility of acceptance and the success of the new leader. The process, done well, is worth the effort.**

If, in order to be successful, a president must have the support (or at least, absence of opposition) of competing constituencies within the campus community, then their participation in the search process is imperative. No matter what the legal authority, it is impossible for a college or university president to be an effective leader without the general consent of the academic community.

The leadership succession process—sometimes prolonged and irritating to those who must conduct it—is calculated to heighten the possibility of acceptance and the success of the new leader. The process, done well, is worth the effort.

Notes

[1] "Statement on Government of Colleges and Universities," *AAUP Bulletin*, Vol. 52, No. 4 (Winter, 1966), pp. 375-379.

[2] Michael D. Cohen and James G. March, *Leadership and Ambiguity: The American College President.* New York: McGraw-Hill, 1974, p. xx.

[3] Harold W. Stoke, *The American College President.* New York: Harper and Row, 1959, p. 20.

[4] J. Victor Baldridge, *Power and Conflict in the University.* New York: John Wiley & Sons, 1971, p. 204.

[5] Michael D. Cohen and James G. March, *op. cit.*, p. 5.

[6] Excerpted from a statement representing a consensus at the December 26, 1973–January 2, 1974 workshop on "Presidential Leadership and University Change," sponsored by the University of Cincinnati and held at Aspen, Colorado, in cooperation with the Aspen Institute for Humanistic Studies.

[7] Michael D. Cohen and James G. March, *op. cit.*, pp. 59-63.

[8] Clark Kerr, "Presidential Discontent," in David C. Nichols (ed.), *Perspectives on Campus Tensions.* Washington, D.C.: American Council on Education, 1970, pp. 139-140.

[9] Michael D. Cohen and James G. March, *op. cit.*, p. 177 and p. 187.

[10] John F. Steiner, *The Presidential Selection Process in Universities.* Dissertation submitted at Graduate College, University of Arizona, 1973.

[11] Robert Birnbaum, "Presidential Succession: An Interinstitutional Analysis," *Educational Record*, Vol. 52, No. 2 (Spring, 1971), p. 135.

[12] Frederic W. Ness, "The Right Time: The Wrong Question," *AGB Reports*, Vol. 13, No. 9 (July-August, 1971), pp. 4-7.

[13] Joseph M. Ray, "In the Middle of the Stream," in Clyde J. Wingfield (ed.), *The American University: A Public Administration Perspective.* Dallas: Southern Methodist University Press, 1970, p. 89.

[14] Robert M. Hyde, "The Presidential Search: Chore or Opportunity?" *Educational Record*, Vol. 50, No. 2 (Spring, 1969), p. 186.

[15] "Statement on Government of Colleges and Universities," *loc. cit.*, p. 377.

[16] Frederic W. Ness, *An Uncertain Glory.* San Francisco: Jossey-Bass, 1971, pp. 60-61.

[17] Robert M. Hyde, *op. cit.*, pp. 186-187.

[18] Paul C. Reinert, S. J., "The Problem With Search Committees," *College Management*, Vol. 9, No. 2, (February, 1974), pp. 10-11, also *AGB Reports*, Vol. 16, No. 7 (April, 1974), pp. 10-15.

[19] John F. Steiner, *op. cit.*

[20] Warren G. Bennis, *The Leaning Ivory Tower.* San Francisco: Jossey-Bass, 1973.

[21] Quoted in Nicholas J. Demerath et al, *Power, Presidents and Professors.* New York: Basic Books, 1967, p. 56.

[22] Manning N. Pattillo, "Choosing a College President," *The Chronicle of Higher Education*, Vol. 7, No. 16 (January 22, 1973), p. 12.

[23] David L. McKenna, "Recycling College Presidents," *Liberal Education*, Vol. 58, No. 4 (December, 1972), pp. 460-461.

[24]J. Stephen Collins, dissertation research project, in progress at Boston College, Department of Higher Education, 1974.

[25]Manning J. Pattillo, *loc. cit.*

[26]Frederick deW. Bolman, *How College Presidents Are Chosen.* Washington, D.C.: American Council on Education, 1965, p. 46.

[27]Louis H. Heilbron, *The College and University Trustee.* San Francisco: Jossey-Bass, 1973, p. 67.

[28]Muriel Beadle, *Where Has All The Ivy Gone?* Garden City: Doubleday & Co., 1972, p. 5.

[29]David L. McKenna, *op. cit.*, p. 462.

[30]Michael D. Cohen and James G. March, *op. cit.*, p. 187.

[31]"Statement on Administrative Leaves," *Liberal Education,* Vol. 57, No. 1 (March, 1971), pp. 88-90.

Bibliography

Books

Beadle, Muriel. *Where Has All The Ivy Gone?* Garden City: Doubleday, Inc., 1972.

Bennis, Warren G. *The Leaning Ivory Tower,* San Francisco: Jossey-Bass, 1973.

Baldridge, J. Victor. *Power and Conflict in the University,* New York: John Wiley & Sons, Inc., 1971.

Bolman, Frederick deW. *How College Presidents Are Chosen,* Washington, D.C.: American Council on Education, 1965.

Cohen, Michael D., and March, James G. *Leadership and Ambiguity: The American College President,* New York: McGraw-Hill, 1974.

Demerath, Nicholas J., Stephens, Richard W., and Taylor, R. Robb. *Power, Presidents and Professors,* New York: Basic Books, 1967.

Dodds, Harold W. *The Academic President – Educator or Caretaker?* New York: McGraw-Hill, 1962.

Ferrari, Michael R. *Profiles of American College Presidents,* East Lansing: Michigan State University Business School, 1970.

Heilbron, Louis H. *The College and University Trustee,* San Francisco: Jossey-Bass, 1973.

Hodgkinson, Harold L. *Institutions in Transition: A Profile of Change in Higher Education,* New York: McGraw-Hill, 1971.

Ingraham, Mark H. *The Mirror of Brass: The Compensation and Working Conditions of College and University Administrators,* Madison: University of Wisconsin Press, 1968.

Kaplowitz, Richard A. *Selecting Academic Administrators: The Search Committee,* Washington, D.C.: American Council on Education, 1973.

Knox, Warren Barr. *Eye of The Hurricane,* Corvallis: Oregon State University Press, 1973.

Ness, Frederic W. *An Uncertain Glory,* San Francisco: Jossey-Bass, 1971.

New York State Regents Advisory Committee. *College and University Presidents: Recommendations and Report of a Survey,* Ithaca: Cornell University, 1967.

Prator, Ralph. *The College President,* Washington, D.C.: The Center for Applied Research in Education, 1963.

Rauh, Morton A. *The Trusteeship of Colleges and Universities,* New York: McGraw-Hill, 1969.

Ritchie, M.A.F. *The College Presidency,* New York: Philosophical Library, 1970.

Stoke, Harold W. *The American College President,* New York: Harper & Row, 1959.

Wingfield, Clyde J. (ed.) *The American University (A Public Administration Perspective),* Dallas: Southern Methodist University Press, 1970.

Articles

Alton, Bruce. "How Long Can a President Serve Effectively?" *College Management,* Vol. 6, No. 11 (Nov., 1971), p. 26.

Auburn, Norman P. "The University Presidency: Mission Impossible?" *Educational Record*, Vol. 52, No. 2 (Spring, 1971), pp. 146-151.

Bennis, Warren G. "Searching For the 'Perfect' College President," *Atlantic*, (April, 1971), pp. 39-53.

Birnbaum, Robert. "Presidential Succession: An Interinstitutional Analysis," *Educational Record*, Vol. 52, No. 2 (Spring, 1971), pp. 133-145.

Bunzel, John H. "Answers From a Presidential Candidate," *Educational Record*, Vol. 52, No. 1 (Winter, 1971), pp. 12-16.

Heady, Ferrel. "The Role of the President Today," *Public Administration Review*, Vol. 30, No. 2 (March/April, 1970), pp. 117-121.

Hyde, Robert M. "The Presidential Search: Chore or Opportunity?" *Educational Record*, Vol. 50, No. 2 (Spring, 1969), pp. 186-188.

Kerr, Clark. "Presidential Discontent," in David C. Nichols (ed.), *Perspectives on Campus Tensions*, Washington, D.C.: American Council on Education, 1970.

Lindahl, Charles W. "Attrition of College Administrators," *Intellect*, (February, 1973), pp. 289-293.

McKenna, David L. "Recycling College Presidents," *Liberal Education*, Vol. 58, No. 4 (Dec., 1972), pp. 456-463.

Nelson, William C. "Administrative Leaves: The Present Status," *Liberal Education*, Vol. 59, No. 3 (October, 1973), pp. 318-324.

Ness, Frederic W. "The Recruitment and Retention of Presidents," *AGB Reports*, Vol. 13, No. 1 (September, 1970), pp. 3-17.

Ness, Frederic W. "The Right Time: The Wrong Question," *AGB Reports*, Vol. 13, No. 9 (July-August, 1971), pp. 4-7.

Pattillo, Manning M. "Choosing a College President," *The Chronicle of Higher Education*, Vol. 7, No. 16 (January 22, 1973), p. 12.

Ray, Joseph M. "Reflections on Presidential Transition (In the Middle of the Stream)," *Public Administration Review*, Vol. 30, No. 2 (March/April, 1970), pp. 125-128.

Reinert, Paul C., S.J. "The Problem With Search Committees," *College Management*, Vol. 9, No. 2 (February, 1974), pp. 10-11, also *AGB Reports*, Vol. 16, No. 7 (April, 1974), pp. 10-15.

Riesman, David. "Vicissitudes in the Career of the College President," speech given at the Dedication of the O. Meredith Wilson Library at University of Minnesota, May 13, 1969.

"Statement on Government of Colleges and Universities," *AAUP Bulletin*, Vol. 52, No. 4 (Winter, 1966), pp. 375-379.

Tunnicliffe, Guy W., and Ingram, John A. "The College President: Who is He?" *Educational Record*, vol. 50, No. 2 (Apring, 1969), pp. 189-193.

Unpublished Dissertation

Steiner, John F. *The Presidential Selection Process in Universities*, Dissertation submitted at Graduate College, University of Arizona, 1973.

Appendix

Five different approaches to the search process for presidents are described below. Highlights of these statements have been presented in the section on "The Search Committee."

Culver-Stockton College, Canton, Missouri, affiliated with the Christian Church (Disciples of Christ).*

The procedures which we used to find and elect a new president for Culver-Stockton College were as follows:

1. Upon receiving the resignation of the former president, who was retiring, the Board appointed 6 of its members to serve as a Presidential Search Committee and designated me as the chairman.

2. The Presidential Search Committee met to discuss the parameters of the problem and to decide on its procedures. In this meeting it was agreed that:
   A. The Board of Directors would elect a new president on the recommendation of the Presidential Search Committee.
   B. Only one candidate would be presented to the Board at a time.
   C. The Search Committee would establish and work closely with a sub-committee made up of students and faculty, with one member of the Presidential Search Committee to serve as liaison between the Presidential Search Committee and the sub-committee for the purpose of reviewing credentials.
   D. We would make no official use of the former president in the work of the committee but that we would consult with him to get the benefit of his knowledge of people under consideration.

3. Immediately following this meeting the committee met with the faculty and explained its procedure as far as it had developed. The faculty was requested to elect three of their members to serve on the sub-committee, which eventually became known as the Screening Committee. They were also requested to submit names of persons they felt should be considered for the presidency, and in the third place they were requested individually to prepare a brief sketch of the qualifications which they felt the new president should have.

---

*This description of procedures was provided by Dr. C. W. Wake, a trustee of Culver-Stockton College and chairman of its search committee. Dr. Wake is, also, a former president of Lynchburg College.

4. The retiring president was asked to arrange with the Student Council or some appropriate body to see that two students were elected to serve on the sub-committee.

5. The Presidential Search Committee and the sub-committee met jointly three times to consider the qualifications that we should expect the new president to have. The sketches submitted by the faculty were reviewed in these meetings and eventually a statement concerning the type of person the committee was looking for evolved. The importance of this phase of the procedure enabled the faculty members, the students and the Trustees to begin to develop a common mind about the presidency of the college and the type of person best suited to serve. The written statement was almost incidental.

6. The description of the person we were looking for was shared with the faculty by the faculty members on the sub-committee and in a later joint meeting of the Presidential Search Committee and the sub-committee faculty reactions were noted and certain changes made.

7. The Presidential Search Committee and the sub-committee then began to look at credentials together. After examining a few we came to an agreement that the sub-committee would continue the screening and that it would turn over to the Presidential Search Committee for further consideration only those names of persons the sub-committee felt would be satisfactory as president of the college, and further, that the sub-committee would explain the reasons for not considering the candidates that they rejected.

8. In several meetings the sub-committee screened from 63 sets of credentials 9 that they felt would be a satisfactory president for the college.

9. In the final joint meeting of the Presidential Search Committee and the sub-committee a general discussion was held concerning these candidates but no effort was made to rank them. The purpose of this meeting was to give the members of the Board a clear feeling of the attitudes and understandings of the faculty with regard to the prospects they were recommending.

10. The Presidential Search Committee met apart from the students and faculty and decided that it wished to interview four of the candidates. Three of the candidates accepted our invitation and engaged in 3-hour interviews with the 6 members of the Presidential Search Committee. The chairman of the committee arranged these interviews and explained to each candidate the

status of the committee's work and that participation in these interviews did not involve any commitment on their part or ours.

11. The Presidential Search Committee quickly decided on the person it wished to present to the Board of Trustees first. Full information was prepared concerning the candidate. A Board meeting was called. The candidate was presented and elected.

Throughout the entire procedure every effort was made to avoid a situation in which the faculty, the students or the Board of Trustees could become fragmented because some supported one candidate and others another. The difficulties that could arise in the college community by a division in or between the faculty, the Board of Trustees and the students was discussed many times and the committee gradually came to a full acceptance of the point of view that its procedures should not only result in the selection of a fine president but should be carried on in such a way as to maintain the solidarity of the entire college community.

Mankato State College, Minnesota, one of seven state colleges in the Minnesota State College System. The State College System is governed by a nine-member Minnesota State College Board. The Chancellor, appointed by that board is the executive officer of the system. The president of Mankato State College is the chief executive officer of that college and is responsible to the board through the Chancellor.

Minnesota State College Board

Administrative Procedure
for the
Selection of a President for Mankato State College

May 22, 1973

I. Purpose

The procedures set forth herein apply to Mankato State College as it participates in the recruitment, nomination, evaluation, and recommendation of presidential candidates for its institution. This procedure, implementing the *Governing Rules* of the Minnesota State College Board, will be in effect until such time as a President for Mankato State College is appointed by the State College Board.

These procedures reflect the commitment of the Board and of the Chancellor to seek the broadest possible involvement of members of Mankato State College and of representatives from the broader campus community. The policy follows in principle the major concepts and patterns employed at St. Cloud State College in 1970 and at Southwest Minnesota State College in 1972, realizing that adaptations are necessary to accommodate differences in local college governance structure and to take advantage of experience acquired in these previous processes.

These guidelines have proved to be extremely valuable in obtaining highly qualified candidates at both St. Cloud and Southwest, and the Board and the Chancellor are confident that the same positive result will occur at Mankato State College.

II. Organization and Composition of the Presidential Search Committee

   A. The college community shall select by June 8, 1973, a Presidential Search Committee which shall serve in an advisory capacity to the Chancellor and the State College Board.
   B. This Committee shall be composed of no more than thirteen persons* who are to represent all components of the college community: teaching faculty (tenured and non-tenured), students, professional support personnel, administrators, and alumni.

   The exact number of representatives from the student, faculty, and professional support personnel components shall be determined through negotiation by the governance bodies for these various components at Mankato State College.

   The Committee shall include one administrator and one alumnus.
   C. Representatives of the students, faculty, and professional support personnel shall be chosen by the respective components through their official agencies for governance.
   D. The administrative representative shall be appointed by President Nickerson (outgoing President) and the alumni representative shall be selected by the Alumni Board.
   E. The membership of the Committee shall also be representative of women and minorities on the campus.
   F. Any member of the Committee who becomes a candidate for the presidential vacancy automatically loses his or her membership and must be replaced.
   G. The Committee will be chaired by the Vice Chancellor for Academic Affairs, who will be a non-voting member, and staffed by a secretary designated by the Vice Chancellor.
   H. President Nickerson shall formally communicate in writing to the Chancellor by June 11, 1973, the names of the members of the Committee.

---

*The search committee membership was expanded from the 13 specified in the procedure to a total of 31. The composition was: 11 faculty, 11 students, 5 professional support personnel, 2 administrators, and 2 alumni.

III. Procedures of the Selection Process

   A. The Search Committee will hold an organizational meeting early in the summer at a time convenient to all members. However, in order to not exclude anyone from the Committee because of summer commitments off-campus or outside of Mankato, the Commitee will not meet again during the summer.

   B. The announcement of the Presidential vacancy and a description of the position shall be circulated broadly throughout the academic community by the Chairman of the Search Committee early in the summer and nominations and applications will be received throughout the summer months.

   Procedures specified for recruitment evaluation, and selection in the Minnesota State College System's affirmative action policy shall be employed to insure the application of minorities and women for the position.

   C. All nominations of persons for the position and all applications shall be made in writing to the Chairman of the Presidential Search Committee. Such persons nominated or applying will be requested to submit their credentials to the Chairman of the Committee no later than September 15, 1973.

   D. The Chairman of the Search Committee shall convene the Search Committee on September 24, 1973. *All credentials* collected during the summer will be made available to the Committee on a confidential basis in a secure office on the campus of Mankato State College. Moreover, during the summer credentials of presidential applicants will be available in the office of the Vice Chancellor for Academic Affairs for members of the Search Committee to review so they may be fully informed and prepared for the evaluation process which will begin in the fall.

   E. By October 5, 1973, the Chairman of the Search Committee, on behalf of the Chancellor, will submit to the Committee from the applications received a list of 20 names for discussion and evaluation by the Committee and will request the written reaction and comments of each member of the Committee.

   Additionally, the Committee may add from any of the applications received any names which at least six members of the Committee desire to have the Chancellor consider further.

   F. By October 12, 1973, comments concerning the qualifications of the list of 20 — and those names added by the Committee — shall be submitted to the Chancellor.

   G. By October 19, 1973, the Chancellor will re-submit 10 names from this list to the Committee for further written comment and evaluation, such comments to be filed with the Chancellor by October 26,

1973. If a majority of the Committee is so inclined, the Committee may include four additional names for comment and evaluation.

H. The Chancellor shall review these comments and the qualifications of the 10 candidates, and shall invite at least three — and more if he chooses for interviews. If a majority of the Committee so recommends, the Chancellor shall invite one or two additional candidates for interviews.

   1. Interviews of each of the candidates shall first be held on the college campus in accordance with procedures established by the Committee. Such interviews will include ample opportunity for representatives of the various campus components to meet with the candidates. An assessment of each candidate may be submitted to the Committee (on the appropriate form provided by the Committee) by each individual involved in the interview process.
   2. After receiving nominations from area legislators, the Governor, the Search Committee, and the President's Community Advisory Council the Chancellor shall select a Regional Advisory Committee composed of not more than eight residents representative of the geographic area which Mankato State College serves. The Regional Advisory Committee shall meet with each of the candidates interviewed for purposes of providing the candidate information on the community which the college serves. Members of the Regional Advisory Committee will also have an opportunity to comment in writing to the Chairman of the Presidential Search Committee concerning their impressions of and reactions to the candidates interviewed.
   3. Each of the candidates shall be interviewed by members of the State College Board and the Chancellor.*

I. Each member of the Presidential Search Committee will comment in writing on the candidates interviewed. These comments, as well as the reactions from the members of the college components and the Regional Advisory Committee, shall be forwarded by the Chairman of the Committee to the Chancellor.

J. By January 1, 1974, the Chancellor will plan to recommend to the Board a nominee for the Presidency of Mankato State College."

---

*Actually, the Board interviews were conducted *publicly* with the news media present. The three finalists were asked basically the same questions in interviews lasting approximately 45 minutes for such candidate. The Board voted by ballot, the votes were tallied, and the results announced. The Board then unanimously passed a motion to name the candidate with a majority of votes as President of Mankato State College.

California State University and Colleges System, comprising nineteen separate campuses under one Board of Trustees.

The title president is used to designate the chief executive officer of each institution in the system. The chancellor of the entire system is the chief executive officer of the board.

Procedures for the Selection of Presidents*

Establishment of Presidential Selection Advisory Committee

Whenever a presidential vacancy arises, a Presidential Selection Advisory Committee ('PSAC') will be established by the Chancellor and the Chairman of the Board of Trustees with representation as follows:
— Campus representation — three members of the campus (the membership and manner of selection determined by the campus)
— Trustee representation — two Trustees to be named by the Chairman of the Board of Trustees
— Presidential representation — one President to be named by the Chancellor
— Advisory Board representation — one member of the Advisory Board to be named by the Advisory Board
— Staff representation — Vice Chancellor, Faculty and Staff Affairs
— Chancellor

Purpose of PSAC

— The PSAC, after thorough review and interview of candidates, will provide a list of acceptable candidates (3-6) for consideration by the Chancellor.
— The Chancellor must recommend at least two nominees to the Board of Trustees. He may submit more than two.

Sources of Candidates

— The PSAC decides from among those nominated who appear most promising for interview by Chancellor and/or Vice Chancellor if they are from out of state. If from in-state, they may be interviewed by the Chancellor and/or Vice Chancellor or by the PSAC. (Results of interviews of those from out of state, and in-state where interviewed by Chancellor or Vice Chancellor, are reported to PSAC. Committee decides then whether to invite them for interview); and
— From pool of promising potential candidates interviewed by Chancellor and/or Vice Chancellor — committee decides after review of vitae and report of interviews on those to invite for PSAC interview.

*Excerpted from a policy document dated August 15, 1973.

Duties of the PSAC

— Restricted solely, after review of background information, to determining whom to interview; interviewing of candidates; and as a result of interviews, determining whom to have investigated fully; and on the basis of interviews and background studies, determining those finalists to be recommended to the Chancellor.
— PSAC decides on basis of vitae and information supplied whom to schedule for interview.
— PSAC interviews candidates scheduled to meet with the committee.
— Results of background studies are shared with PSAC. PSAC decides on basis of interviews and background studies those finalists to be recommended to the Chancellor.
— All checking and contacts with candidates is handled by the Vice Chancellor for Faculty and Staff Affairs, and his staff. No contacts are to be made directly with candidates by other members of the PSAC. No personal or letter checks are to be made by members of the PSAC with individuals at a candidate's current or past places of employment.

Confidentiality

There is to be no campus committee nor any consultation with those on campus by campus representatives on PSAC. Any departure from the provisions for confidentiality or the prohibition against independent checking on those being considered by the committee can be cause for the PSAC to be abolished and the function taken over by a special Trustee committee.

Final Stages of Selection Process

— Candidates will, whenever possible, visit campus prior to appearing before the Board of Trustees.
— Campus representatives on PSAC will handle arrangements for campus visit and will do everything possible to (1) make it clear that campus visit is *not* a part of the PSAC screening and selection process and (2) maintain as much security as possible during and after campus visits.

University of Wisconsin, comprising twenty-seven campus units, with a single governing board (Board of Regents). In this system the campus heads are designated chancellors and the head of the entire system is called president.

The board approved procedures for selecting chancellors is as follows:
1. Upon indication of such vacancy, the President of the Board would promptly designate a Special Regent Committee to be involved in

the selection process for a replacement consisting of not less than three nor more than five Regents. The Board President would designate a chairman of the Special Committee.

2. The Special Committee would then confer with the President of the System and advise him at that point of any special qualifications for the position which they felt should be considered. In essence, the Special Committee would work with the System President to produce a brief job description taking into account the special characteristics of the institution at which the Chancellor would serve or the special characteristics of the administrative position to be occupied.

3. The System President would then appoint a Search and Screen Committee comprised of:
    a. A majority of faculty, selected by the System President after consultation with appropriate faculty representatives.
    b. Students and administrators.
    c. A chairman shall be appointed by the System President from among the faculty members of the Committee.

    The Search and Screen Committee would be provided with the job description prepared by the System President and the Special Committee. Interviews of candidates by the Search and Screen Committee will be within the discretion of that Committee.

4. The Search and Screen Committee would subsequently return a list to the System President of at least five individuals that they felt were qualified in unranked order along with an alphabetical list of all persons considered. Delivery of the list shall be at a joint meeting of the Search and Screen Committee, the System President and the Special Committee in order that the System President and the Special Committee can receive an oral presentation on each of the candidates recommended. The Search and Screen Committee would then be discharged, provided that if no person contained in the initial list presented by the Search and Screen Committee is found acceptable, then the Search and Screen Committee shall be reactivated and asked to provide a second list of at least five additional candidates.

5. The System President, in conjunction with the Special Committee, would review all of the recommended candidates and interview those they desired. The System President would then make his recommendation to the Special Committee which in turn would make its report on the System President's recommendation to the Board.

6. Final approval of the System President's selection shall be made by the Board of Regents.

Knox College, * Galesburg, Illinois (private), As finally constituted the Knox Search Committee was a large one of seven appointed trustees, two ex officio trustees, three faculty members and two students. At my request, the Acting President of the College joined the Committee as an active advisor and consultant. In essence, therefore, the Committee membership numbered 15.

The geographical distribution and the work schedules of the members made frequent — or even regular — meetings impossible. Phone calls and memoranda had to suffice. As time went on those members in Galesburg became a "campus" sub-committee and did the substantial part of information gathering and reference checking.

For Knox this worked well — the reason being the loyalty, dedication, and responsibility of the individual members.

Two assignments were given to the Committee by the Trustees:
1. To recommend at the June 1 and 2 meetings of the Trustees an Acting President to serve until a permanent President was elected and took office.
2. To search for and recommend to the Trustees the candidate best qualified to lead Knox at this time and in the years ahead.

The first meeting of the entire Committee was held June 1, and after full discussion it was agreed that Hermann R. Muelder, former Dean of the College and a highly respected faculty member and scholar, be recommended to the Trustees as the Acting President. The Trustees accepted this recommendation and the first assignment was completed.

On June 2, 1973, the Committee reconvened and, in general, decided on the *modus operandi* to be followed.

The most important aspects of the task — other than the search per se — were thought to be the determination of the kind of leader needed, the establishing of a budget, the setting up of clerical procedures and the projection of a time table for accomplishment.

So far as leadership qualities were concerned, it was decided that the present needs of Knox required a president:
1. Who could develop an 'exciting' concept of liberal arts at Knox. The development of such a concept had to come from his/her own belief in the small liberal arts college and from his/her recognition that Knox has a superior base for building an exciting and 'century ahead' program of liberal arts.
2. Who could communicate effectively the 'excitement' of liberal arts — and the Knox program — to all related publics.

---

*This description of the search process conducted by Knox College in 1973-74 was provided by the Chairman of their Presidential Search Committee, Trustee Scott Harrod.

3. Who could — because of his/her own self-induced enthusiasm for liberal arts — be an effective fund raiser.
(Note: As time went on the Committee recognized that this third requirement should be expanded to include effective recruitment of students.)

Obviously, a successful candidate should have academic credentials, administrative interest and capability, great energy, integrity and the commonly agreed upon characteristics of leadership.

So far as the budget was concerned, an amount of $20,000 was established.

To set up clerical routines and procedures, one of the committee members was named recorder.

A tentative time table was established to have front running candidates identified by the October Board meeting and to have a candidate recommendation by the winter meeting of the Trustees.

During June, July and August of 1973, substantial efforts were made to obtain the names of qualified and potential candidates. To this end an article appeared in the KNOX ALUMNUS requesting help. A letter went to about 1300 students and parents. In addition, about 700 special letters individually addressed, went to trustees, faculty, staff, alumni in higher education, alumni achievement award winners, honorary degree recipients, ACM presidents, other college presidents, donors and foundations and organizations concerned with higher education.

From these efforts the Committee received approximately 290 names for consideration. The Committee then followed the routine described below:

1. The Committee gathered available data from biographical sources on the suggested names and started a file on each name. A thank you letter went to the one who suggested the name.
2. The preliminary biographical data so obtained were forwarded to each member of the Committee for an initial reaction on an 'A,' 'B,' 'C' basis.
3. From the 290 suggested names 48 received Committee grades warranting further investigation.
4. By the end of October screening was sufficiently far along to permit the selection of names for first contacts and interviews. All together twelve candidates were interviewed by at least two members of the Committee.
5. As the result of the interviewing process, four prospective candidates were invited to the campus. One withdrew before a campus visit but three spent — at different times — about a day and a half in Galesburg meeting faculty, staff, and students.

From time to time during the screening process described above, the Committee, either in meeting or by phone, engaged in an informal ranking and comparison of the candidates being considered. While the names did change somewhat, it became generally evident that a relatively few stayed at the top and that the majority ranking was consistently the same.

This was evident at the December 15 meeting of the Committee when there was also realization that time was running out if a recommendation was to be made to the Trustees at the Winter meeting. To expedite the work of the Committee, a three-member 'Action Sub-Committee' was empowered to act for the Committee in the final discussions with the leading candidates.

The action of this sub-committee culminated in the selection of a candidate ratified by the Committee through a telephone poll. The recommended candidate was appointed President by the Trustees in February, 1974, to take office as of July 1, 1974.

28